THE
ROAD

The Road – A Guide to Crossing the
Nepal Himalayas by Bike
Published in Great Britain in 2024 by Graffeg Limited.

Text: Richard Williams copyright © 2024.
Photography: Manish Maharjan (Section 1)
and Ananta Poudel (Section 2).
Cartography: Mark Murphy.
Guide: Om Adhikari.
Contributing Writer: Jenny Caunt.
Maps: © OpenStreetMap 2024.
Shutterstock photos: pages 46, 47, 160, 262.

Graffeg Limited, 24 Stradey Park Business
Centre, Mwrwg Road, Llangennech, Llanelli,
Carmarthenshire, SA14 8YP, Wales, UK.
www.graffeg.com.

Richard Williams is hereby identified as the author
of this work in accordance with section 77 of the
Copyright, Designs and Patents Act 1988.

A CIP Catalogue record for this book is available
from the British Library.

ISBN 9781802586640

1 2 3 4 5 6 7 8 9

A Guide to Crossing the Nepal
Himalayas by Bike

THE
ROAD

Richard Williams
Photography Manish Maharjan
and Ananta Poudel
Cartography Mark Murphy
Contributing writer Jenny Caunt
Guide Om Adhikari

GRAFFEG

Contents

Part 2
Preparing for your Trip

Part 3
The Route and Guidebook

Contents

Interviews

Interviews with the Gamechangers

Interviews with International Riders

Foreword

Photo by Michal Cerveny.

The rise of adventure cycling worldwide in recent years has been nothing short of remarkable. After decades of only two core dominant cycling disciplines – road cycling and mountain biking – two new forms of bicycle riding have recently emerged which are rapidly transforming the sport and allowing greater access for riders to more adventurous environments – gravel biking and e-biking.

The gravel bike, a tougher kind of road bike built for more intrepid riding, has opened up a whole new world of possibilities in adventure for the traditional road cyclist.

The second new form of bicycle, the e-bike, has become nothing short of a revolution in the sport of cycling. E-bikes have changed how we ride and our perception of what is possible on a bicycle. These cutting-edge yet simple off-road machines have made mountain biking accessible to all ages and all levels of fitness with their seamless electrical assistance.

Along with traditional hardtail and full-suspension mountain bikes, the gravel and e-bike have made mountain ranges worldwide more accessible, and riders are flocking to them, from the Alps to the Rockies to the Andes.

In 2017, I acted as an ambassador and competitor in a mountain bike race in Colombia, La Leyenda del Dorado – a gruelling six-day mountain bike stage race through the Colombian Andes. During the race I noticed a very uncomfortable-looking 26-inch-wheeled bike, the only one in the race, and wondered who would ride such a thing. It turned out to be Richard's bike. Over the race days we struck up a friendship over our love of the Colombian mountains and especially the country's exceptional coffee. Richard and his race partner, Tom, would always pass the finish line late in the day, but they always wore big smiles, having had a fabulous day of adventure riding through the mountains. It was clear to me that these guys encapsulated the spirit of cross-country mountain biking. They were not in it to win it, but to soak up the experience and spirit of adventure and to enjoy the feeling only a cyclist knows, out there in the elements, both on and off the bike. They crossed the line safely each day, having ridden diligently, with an attitude of self-preservation.

When Richard told me about his project to cross the Nepal Himalayas by bike and to document it with this guidebook, I knew he would find an accessible and safe route that would not be too technically challenging, therefore opening up The Road to many demographics of cyclist. Then, the more I looked into The Road, the more I wanted to ride it myself. So, in late November 2023, I travelled to Nepal for the first time and rode the second section of The Road on my gravel bike, with Canadian professional mountain biker Cory Wallace as my riding buddy. I was blown away not only by the extraordinary riding, but by the warm hospitality Cory and I received everywhere we went, from the minute we landed until the moment we left. Whether cycling in the hustle and bustle of Kathmandu or riding in a remote village in the distant hills, the welcome was incredible and completely sincere.

The Road is not for the faint-hearted. The climbs and the descents are literally 'next level' compared to the riding roads in the European Alps, and the scale of the mountains will take your breath away as you traverse staggering ridges with soaring 8,000m Himalayan peaks as your backdrop. You will need stamina and determination to make it through each day, but the joy and magic of new discoveries around every corner or over every hilltop will bring you waves of fresh energy that will keep you pedalling forward. The road surface is good overall and non-technical, suitable for experienced gravel riders, mountain bikers and even e-bikers.

Richard's book serves as a comprehensive guide to crossing the middle Himalaya range of Nepal, as well as providing informative and passionate words and anecdotes of the country and its beautiful people. We hope The Road will attract more cyclists and provide a source of sustainable income to some of the poorest and most remote communities in the Himalayas.

If you are looking for a once-in-a-lifetime cycling adventure in a challenging but safe environment through the mother of all mountain ranges, look no further than The Road.

Christoph Sauser
Olympic medalist, four-time World Champion and five-time Cape Epic winner.

Preface

I fell into mountain biking by chance. It began in 2000, a few kilometres outside the remote Himalayan town of Leh, nestled within the sparse region of Ladakh in the northwest of India. I was travelling with two school friends, Sam and Louy.

We'd been hiking between the monasteries and gompas of the region and were blown away by the landscape – a spectacular lunar-like realm of barren, snow-dusted mountains, separated by gaping valleys gouged deep into the Earth like nothing I'd seen before.

We had flown to Leh from Delhi, bouncing through the clouds on an old Alliance Air 737 that had springy paisley seats and wooden drop-down tabletops. Not being too comfortable in the sky, Sam and I were happy that we would be returning back to civilisation by road, via the Leh to Manali Highway, billed as 'the world's highest motorable road.' We hadn't given much thought to this upcoming journey, other than excited anticipation.

That excitement dissipated less than ten minutes into the trip when we heard a hard repetitive slapping noise outside the bus window, which after a minute or so prompted the driver to swing us off the road. He and his co-pilot leaped off and started a commotion with some locals there on the town's dusty outskirts, all centred around one of the bus's back tyres.

The local passengers shuffled off soon after, seemingly in the knowledge we would not be restarting the trip anytime soon. The three of us followed.

The problem was that the tread had come undone from the tyre on one of the rear wheels and lay on the floor like a flattened black eel – not the most encouraging start to the two-day drive over the world's highest road.

Through a mixture of concern and anxiety, we quickly inspected the other tyres of the bus and found them all to be bald. Some even had wire coming through them.

The damaged tyre was fixed with wallpaper paste-like glue from an old, damaged paint pot that was magically at hand and spread on with a flat piece of wood. The co-pilot then pressed the tread back onto the tyre for around five minutes and gave two thumbs up when it was clear the rubber had stuck back on. Brand new.

Outskirts of Pokhara.

Together we discussed if it was a good idea to get back on the bus. Considering the antiquated 737 option and the fact that a number of our fellow bus passengers were Buddhist monks (who after inspection did not have a look of death on their faces), we stepped back onto the vehicle and ran the most terrifying gauntlet for two full days, up and over some of the world's highest mountain passes – up over 5000m – and down into gorges that felt like we were descending into the belly of the Earth.

Naively, we had taken the first two rows of seats on the bus, which were positioned some distance ahead of the front wheels. This meant we were thrust over the verge on virtually every corner and hairpin bend, each one taken wildly by our driver, who we nicknamed Fast Hands for his ability to manoeuvre the bends at an ungodly speed. The co-pilot was barely needed.

Rice fields, Central Nepal.

For those two long days we gaped in horror down at shear 1000m+ drops into abyss after abyss and we hardly spoke a word.

Midway through the highway, just after we descended the Gata Loops – a series of twenty-one death defying hairpin bends – we spotted something that we had not seen for days – westerners... on bikes.

Mountain bikes. Of course! What the hell were we doing on this bus?

We made a pact there and then – to ride the Leh-Manali Highway one day on mountain bikes (which not one of us owned at that point). It took us five years, but we rode it in 2005, and a love affair with mountain biking in the Himalayas was born. Soon after, we ventured to the eastern Indian Himalayas, to Darjeeling and Sikkim.

Some years later, in 2013, I was looking for a challenge and came across the Yak Attack – the world's highest mountain bike race. I saw that it was a circumnavigation of the famous Annapurna Circuit hiking route in Nepal, which I had walked back in 1998. Knowing the terrain and the altitude considerations I decided to sign up.

The Yak Attack was a wonderful experience and one of the toughest imaginable. It helped that the fellow riders were an eclectic ensemble of like-minded people and we all got through it together, dragged on by the top Nepalese mountain bikers at the front of the pack. In such an event (two weeks together in quite extreme conditions) strong relationships were forged and good friends made.

Two years later the earthquake struck Nepal and the horror stories began to filter through. Some of the riders I had become friends with during Yak Attack and their families had been badly affected, so I made an effort to try to raise some money to help rebuild a group of schools in a rural area near the epicentre of the earthquake where some of the boys came from. I have been going back to Nepal almost every year since.

The smoky middle Himalayan mountains and foothills are completely mesmerising and so vast that they seem to go on forever. To see life played out in the countless remote communities, many with their own unique customs and ways developed over centuries in isolation, is a warm and humbling experience. People work hard, life is tough, but there is an infectious happiness in the peoples of the foothills, where material wealth is almost non-existent. And there is rarely a dull moment.

The path chosen for The Road is an adventurous, but fun and culturally rich route – not dangerous or technically difficult (but there is a lot of climbing – there's no avoiding that!). The Road is mostly paved, so it is accessible for mountain bikers with intermediate skills, experienced gravel riders and even intrepid e-bikers, who could conquer The Road with careful planning.

The route will flood your senses at every turn and create memory after memory that will last a lifetime. All you need is an appetite for adventure, a passion for endurance and an open mind and you'll be all set for the ultimate cycling journey across the rooftop of the world.

Richard Williams

Jajarkot.

PART 1
Introduction

Once-in-a-Lifetime Adventure

This is a guidebook for anyone who enjoys riding a bike and is looking for a once-in-a-lifetime adventure – cycling across the Himalayan mountains of Nepal.

It is not a guide for an extreme mountain biking journey up amongst the snow-capped 8,000m-high Himalayan peaks, but rather an achievable way to weave across the entire country through an old mountain trading route that is now being developed into the Mid Hills High Road through the Middle Himalayan Range, which stretches all the way across the breadth of the country of Nepal from west to east.

Dusty hills, the Mid-West.

Along The Road you will encounter rural Nepali life unchanged for hundreds of years as you traverse exotic valleys locked away in a remote and mountainous land that time forgot. You will stop for endless cups of chai, plates of dal bhat and bowls of noodle soup as you share a moment in a small village with a contented community that will be as intrigued by you as you will be by them. Learn a few words and try to understand regional customs and courtesies. You will get blisters, chapped lips, sore legs, aching joints and no doubt some sunburn, but the joy you will feel peddling into a remote Nepali village at sundown to a warm fire, a hot dinner and big encouraging smiles will make those pains dissipate in a heartbeat as you build your body up again with food and rest for the following day's adventure. And that is what The Road is – an adventure, an experience of a lifetime through the heart of one of planet Earth's most spectacular natural arenas.

Map of The Road

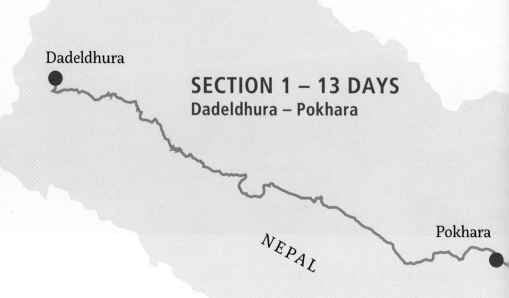

Dadeldhura

SECTION 1 – 13 DAYS
Dadeldhura – Pokhara

NEPAL

Pokhara

The Road is broken up into two sections:

Section 1 runs from the far western town of Dadeldhura through to the beautiful lakeside town of Pokhara in central Nepal. This section runs through some of the most remote settlements and communities in Nepal, where western travellers are very rarely seen. The western regions are also some of the poorest in the country, but the people are among the kindest and most curious you are ever likely to encounter.

The Road is mostly paved, with some sections of unpaved track scattered all along it. There are some huge climbs and epic descents, making each day a pick 'n' mix of experiences that will keep your senses tingling as you traverse eastwards.

Section 2 begins in Pokhara and takes you through the remote central Mid Hills of Nepal, a region steeped in history and tradition. In this region, western travellers are a little more frequent, but as you head further east you will enter more remote and uncharted rural areas, where your arrival on bikes will be viewed with warm and friendly curiosity. The far east is rich in culture, especially the territories of the Rai and Limbu people, where local clothing and architecture are particularly vibrant. The riding out east becomes quite spectacular, with frequent views of the high Himalayan range as a backdrop to the never-ending rollercoaster that takes you up and over the exhilarating Mid Hills and all the way to the end of The Road, the small mountain town of Phidim.

SECTION 2 – 16 DAYS
Pokhara – Phidim Bazaar

Kathmandu

NEPAL

Phidim
Bazaar

Hindu shrine, the Far West.

NEPAL A Brief Overview

Nepal is a mountainous landlocked country in south Asia, bordered by India and China. Much of the country is located in the Himalayan mountain range, with eight of the ten highest mountains in the world, including the world's highest mountain – Mount Everest (8848m). The country occupies 88,041km and has a population of just over 30 million at the time of publication. The country has a traditional economic system whereby three quarters of the population still engage in subsistence farming activities.

There is huge ethnic diversity in Nepal. In the lower valley regions around Kathmandu and Pokhara reside predominantly Indo-Aryan and Tibeto-Burman speaking people. In the Himalayan highlands live predominantly ethnic people of Mongolian-origin, speaking Tibetan and other Tibeto-Burman languages, including the legendary Sherpa people. In the southern section of the country along the low-lying and fertile flatlands of the Terai region lives a significant percentage of the country's population, mainly of Indo-Aryan descent. For more information on the different ethnic and regional groups of Nepal see page 37.

Central Nepal.

Nepal has a rich history dating back to the 8th or 7th century BC, with the arrival of the Kirati people from the east. Later, in the late 6th century BC, the philosophy of Buddhism was conceived in Lumbini, Nepal, by Siddhartha Gautama – the Buddha – and spread throughout the country. By around 200 AD, Hinduism had largely supplanted Buddhism and continued to dominate the country through various Hindu dynasties and kingdoms over subsequent centuries.

East Nepal.

Typical rural home, Central Nepal.

Gathering rice.

In the mid- to late eighteenth century, King Prithvi Narayan Shah, the renowned Gorkha king and warrior, unified the territories of Nepal, creating what is now considered modern Nepal. He became the first monarch of the Kingdom.

In modern times, Nepal has been beset with ongoing political turmoil (most notably between 1996-2006) due to an armed Maoist insurgency. In 2006, the country's monarchy was abolished. In 2008, a republic was declared. After a lengthy peace process, a new republican constitution was promulgated in 2015.

Due to this period of political instability, as well as the impact of the devastating earthquake in 2015, Nepal's development has lagged behind many other developing countries, and today it remains one of the poorest countries in the world.

In more recent years the economy has begun a steady shift away from agriculture with a significant migration from rural to urban areas and overseas. Approximately 4-6 million Nepalis now work abroad, mostly in the Gulf states. Today the Nepali service sector contributes over 50% of the country's GDP.

Taking a break, the Far West.

The History of Mountain Biking in Nepal

While traditional cycling in Nepal had been around for many years, the first mountain bikes (without suspension) were introduced in 1987 by a keen local adventurer named Sonam Gurung. Sonam rode his first mountain bike all the way to Everest Base Camp and back to his hometown of Manang, which opened people's eyes to the potential of this new type of bicycle. Two years later, the first front suspension mountain bikes arrived in Nepal.

In 1990, an American lady named Francis Higgins created Nepal's first mountain biking company, Himalayan Mountain Bike (HMB), which was subsequently taken over three years later by fellow American James Giambrone. James introduced bicycle hire and day tours with guides Lokesh Chandra Sharma, Jeet Bahadur Tamang, and Sonam Gurung as a mechanic and guide. Two years after that, overnight mountain bike trips were introduced to Nagarkot to capture sunset and sunrise views over the spectacular mountain landscape.

During the early 90s, the same team created the first mountain bike race in Nepal, from Kakani – Scar Route – Budhanilkantha. It was called the Himalayan Mountain Bike Championship, and it was mostly a single-track event. In 1994, the inaugural Annapurna Triathlon was organised. It consisted of a 2km swim, 55km bike ride and a 15km run. Due to the rough terrain, mountain bikes were used instead of road bikes for the bike leg. After the successful event in Pokhara, a triathlon was held in Kathmandu – swimming at Phora Durbar, cycling one full lap of the city's ring road, and running from Phora Durbar to Hattigauda and back.

With a forward momentum led by Sonam's Gurung's cousin – the cyclist and adventurer Chhimi Gurung – there was a push to formally recognise mountain biking as a national sport. Chhimi's efforts paid off, and in 1995, mountain biking was welcomed into the Nepali Sports Council, and in the same year the Nepal Mountain Bike Association was formed, with links to international bodies UCI and

Asian Cycling Confederation. Four years later the name was changed to Nepal Cycling Association (NCA) to be inclusive to all forms of cycling.

The sport developed slowly and organically over the next decade until 2007, when Chhimi teamed up with English mountain biker Phil Evans (interview, page 291) to create the Yak Attack, a pioneering multi-day stage race in the extreme environment surrounding the Annapurna Himalayas. Yak Attack aimed to put the Nepali Himalayas firmly on the global mountain biking map. The event was a success and Yak Attack, the world's highest mountain bike race (highest point 5416m!), is still today regarded as one of the toughest races on the planet and features regularly in international mountain bike magazines and media.

In 2008, Nepali mountain biking took a big step forward by putting a team forward for the 14th Asian Mountain Bike championships held in Chobhar, Nepal. Sixteen countries and over one hundred and seventy participants took part in the cross-country (XCO) and Downhill categories. This exposure in the international arena was a revolution for the Nepali mountain biking community and the spectacle triggered a wave of new generation mountain bike riders and put Nepal firmly on the map. As a result, some trekking companies began to add mountain biking to their portfolio of tours and new mountain biking companies began to set up shop alongside Himalayan Mountain Bike (HMB), the most prominent being Chhimi Gurung's Dawn Till Dusk, which worked to attract large numbers of budding mountain bikers from Europe and North America, who returned home with tales of mystical adventures in the far-flung and remote Himalayan mountains.

Today, mountain biking is not only a growing source of income for the Nepali tourism industry, it also provides many jobs to young Nepali's who work as guides, mechanics, shop workers and drivers. Exploration of new riding areas continues at pace by the huge scene of riders who see the opportunity to make Nepal a mecca for mountain biking.

Some Nepali riders, most notably Ajay Pandit Chhetri (interview, page 265) have gone on to compete internationally at the highest level and win trophies and accolades in Europe, North and South America, inspiring the next generation of riders back home on the trails and in the bike shops of Kathmandu and Pokhara.

The rise of female participation in the sport has been one of the most positive developments in recent years. Due to cultural and caste

considerations whereby girls and young women have historically often been prohibited from such activities, the new generation of trailblazing female riders have broken down many barriers and stereotypes and made it OK for girls to go out, ride bikes, make a living, and have fun.

The first lady mountain biker and cross-country competitor was Nirjala Tamrakar the 'Mountain Queen,' who dominated the sport from 2001 for over twelve years. Nirjala's success inspired the next wave of talented riders, most notably Laxmi Magar (interview, page 270) and more recently Usha Khanal (interview, page 278). In the more technical and dangerous discipline of enduro riding, Nishma Shrestha (interview, page 283) has paved the way for female riders to really go over the edge.

Still, the ratio of female to male riders remains very small at the time of publication, but more events and initiatives like the Ladies Mountain Biking League 'mountain bike library' for novice female riders to try out the sport for free with on-loan equipment are having a positive impact.

The future for Nepali mountain biking looks bright.

Under Kanchenjunga.

Central Nepal.

After a number of difficult years following the 2015 earthquake, the sport has bounced back with more momentum than ever with an explosion of events and tourist numbers increasing with each new season.

Nepali riders are also pushing themselves to go deeper into the mountains in the name of exploration and discovery. In 2022, local mountain biker and guide Mangal Lama (interview, page 287) completed the first mountain bike traverse of the mythical Great Himalayan Trail (GHT), a high-altitude hiking route that spans the entire Nepal Himalaya from east to west. The GHT has only been completed by a small number of elite individuals on foot.

In terms of pushing physical limits, Canadian professional mountain biker, Cory Wallace (interview, page 296), has completed several circumnavigations of the high altitude 215km-long Annapurna Circuit in under 24 hours; a route that typically takes four to five days even for the fittest mountain bikers. Mangal and Cory's achievements on their mountain bikes have shifted the goalposts of what is possible in cross-country mountain biking in the Himalayas.

There has also been a surge in exploration of new enduro trails in the east of Nepal led by Kathmandu guide and co-owner of Himalayan Single Track Santosh Rai (interview page 273). Enduro riding is exploding, particularly with the younger generation of Nepali mountain bikers, so in the years ahead there is expected to be a huge range of enduro options in Nepal, including uplifts by jeep, cable car and even helicopter.

The floodgates are now firmly open for more remote and extreme mountain bike adventures in the Nepali Himalayas into the exciting years ahead.

Cobbled Streets,
Central Nepal.

THE COUNTRY OF NEPAL
What to Expect

When most people think of Nepal they think of Mount Everest, extreme mountaineering, treacherous mountain roads, eye-watering flights in ramshackle planes, Gurkha soldiers, yaks and yetis, all set in the romantic yet foreboding arena of the world's highest mountains, the Himalayas.

While most of these things exist, the typical cyclist to Nepal will not experience the risk that this perception of high-altitude adventure suggests. While the terrain certainly throws up many physical challenges, the Nepali people live and function in harmony within their dramatic environment, harnessing and utilising their land to their benefit, mostly through the fertile, lower lying foothills and lowlands of the country, an area perfectly set-up for challenging and culturally immersive cycling.

The majority of settlements can be found on hilltops or near to water, amongst the vast network of surging rivers that drain down from the high mountains to the lush valley floors, where most life, and trails, can be found. This means riding lots of ups and lots of downs between villages. This requires a good level of grit and endurance going up, and an inclination for thrills going down.

While the vast majority of cycling trips to Nepal are problem free through careful planning, professional guiding and diligent riding, do not forget, Nepal can be a hostile place when the weather takes a turn for the worse, or if you fall off your bike with a serious injury. Floods and landslides are common in the monsoon season, and at other times with increasingly volatile weather patterns. Rural health services are basic, and you could be a number of hours from a well-equipped hospital. So plan well, and ride safe.

An Overview of the Nepali People

From arrival in Kathmandu airport, after you have passed the eager but polite taxi drivers and porters, you will typically be greeted with a warm welcome and the most genuine hospitality by some of the kindest people you have ever met. As you venture out into the more remote parts of the country on your adventure you will feel this welcome deepen further and a connection to the country of Nepal and its people will undoubtedly develop.

From an early age, Nepali's are encouraged to treat foreign travellers with respect and kindness. Tourism remains an important industry in Nepal and one of its largest sources of foreign exchange and revenue. While trekking and mountaineering still make up the majority of foreign visitors, mountain biking and cycling is catching up steadily with a rapid increase in companies specialising in bike tours, and there has been a real effort by Nepali mountain bikers to go out and discover new mountain biking and cycling trails all over the country in an attempt to broaden the appeal of Nepal to all kinds of mountain bikers and cyclists.

With eight of the ten highest mountains on Earth, Nepal can be considered as the rooftop of the world. For decades, it has been the Holy Grail destination for mountaineers seeking the ultimate challenge and adventure. For these adventures to be possible, a strong contingent of local sherpas, porters, guides, logisticians and support staff has always been required. The same goes for cycle trips in the mountains. Due to the challenging nature of most adventure trips in Nepal, it is highly recommended

that you recruit a cycling guide with experience in, and knowledge of, the regions you will travel through. In addition to this, a support vehicle to carry all necessary supplies and camping gear can also help to maximise your experience riding freely on your bike through the Middle Himalayas.

Once you have established your team, camaraderie will develop swiftly and strong bonds will form between you as the visitor and your Nepali hosts. While there is a strong sense of 'we are in this together,' encouraged by the humble nature of your Nepali team, never forget to always listen, and to follow your guide's instructions and recommendations at all times. You will never know better than them.

The Nepali's are enterprising people and can fix most problems themselves (or know a man/woman who can). From minor to major bike repairs or injuries, to sourcing food and cold beer in the wilderness, you will be staggered by your guide's ability to find a solution to the numerous issues you may encounter during your trip.

The People of Far West and Mid West Nepal

The western regions of Nepal along the Mid Hills – the route of The Road, has very few western visitors, so there is currently very

Dailekh District.

little tourist infrastructure between the far west and Pokhara. This means international tourists are not a common sight. People will be curious of western faces, but always friendly. It may take a while for locals to acknowledge you, but be kind, say Namaste with your hands pressed together and smile, and you should receive a big smile in return. The kids in the west and midwest are particularly enthusiastic to see foreigners and will likely try to engage you with laughter and possibly try to borrow your bike for a quick peddle around the Bazaar.

The People of Central and Eastern Nepal

Once you approach Pokhara and central Nepal, you are in more developed and established tourist territories. These continue all the way east, around the Kathmandu Valley, past Langtang, Makalu and Everest regions to the eastern border, where The Road ends. In the high Himalayan regions, the locals are very much used to the many foreign visitors that come to climb and trek in the mountains, and English is widely spoken, along with other languages. However, The Road route through the Middle Himalayas remains a path much less trodden and people are still not used to a throughflow of foreign travellers. Many people in the more remote parts of central and eastern Nepal will still be curious, but always friendly and happy to assist you whenever you need guidance or help.

Local lady, Dailekh District.

Cultural and Ethnic Groups of Nepal

Nepal's population of almost 30 million is a melting pot of multi-ethnic diversity which comes from three main groups, Indo-Nepalese, Tibeto-Nepalese and Indigenous Nepalese.

From the outside looking in, the culture and society here can be multi-layered and confusing. There are up to 126 castes/ethnic groups in Nepal, each with their own sub-groups, languages, social norms and cultural practices.

Here is an overview of some of the better-known ethnic groups of Nepal you may come across during the Trans-Nepal Journey.

Brahmins

The name Brahmin is anglicised from the Sanskrit word *Brahmana*, which means 'Supreme self'. Brahmins are considered as the highest of the castes in Nepal. Brahmins, along with Chhetris, have played a leading role in the forming of Nepal as a modern state. They make up about 40% of the government and administrative workforce.

While there are many sub-groups of Brahmins, the ones you will encounter most along 'The Road' are the Hill Brahmins, found in the central parts of Nepal. Their main tongue is Nepali and they are considered to be more educated, holding positions in villages as teachers and priests as well as being farmers.

Chhetri

Chhetri people are believed to have migrated to Nepal from medieval India. They occupy a lot of the Mid-Hill regions of central eastern Nepal. They dominated the high military positions and monopolised the military forces from the 1840s onwards as the administrators and governors. Chhetri is the most populous ethnic group in Nepal.

Gurung

Gurung people are found in the Gandaki Province of Nepal and live around Pokhara, Manang, the lower foothills of Annapurna. They form one of the main Gurkha tribes and historically served the Shah kings as mercenaries. In 1769, they played a significant role in the campaign to

The Far West.

unify Nepal under Prithvi Narayan, whose palace/fort you can find in Gorkha.

They migrated to Nepal from Tibet via Manang. Originally, they practiced Bon and Tibetan Buddhism and later on, as they mixed with other ethnic groups, they began to practice Hinduism.

Magar

The Magar are the third most prolific of Nepal's ethnic groups by population. Their primary sources of income are agriculture and military service, predominantly as Gurkha soldiers. More traditionally, they are known as craftsmen, blacksmiths and bridge builders. The northern Magar people are predominantly Buddhist, while those found in the southern regions tend towards Hinduism. On this journey you will mostly find these people in the Western Regions.

While there are many mythical stories about the origins of the Magars, it is believed their history can be traced back to 1100.

One of the stories tells of an unknown woman that appears one day from an unknown village and has a son. This son then grows up and catches an angel while she is drinking. He married the angel, they had three sons who went on to become the forefathers of three of the four the major Magar clans (Buddha, Roka and Gharti). The founder of the fourth clan was discovered by a young shepherd. One of his goats disappeared each day, only to return later. He followed it and found the goat had been giving her milk to a boy child. The shepherd raised the boy, and the boy became the forefather of the Jhankari clan.

Tharu

You will come across the Tharu people most likely while travelling to the start point of The Road. They consider themselves as the first people of Nepal and direct descendants of Guatum Buddha. You find them in the Terai or flatlands down near the border of India. Tharu's physical features resemble more that of the Aryan people of India rather than the Mongolian features of the hill people.

Tamang

Many believe the word *tamang* means 'horse' (*ta*) and warrior (*mak*) in Tibetan, and certainly the Tamangs have been involved in many battles in the history of Nepal, not as conquering heroes but as undesirables to be conquered. Though they are native to Nepal, Tamangs have prehistoric and genetic roots that can be traced through Tibet and Mongolia which is why other ethnic groups refer to them as Bhote, which means outsiders or those hailing from the high regions.

Occupying over 50% of Nepal's hill regions, the Tamangs were seen as an inferior and threatening race by other Hindu Castes who were intimidated by their greater numbers. Even in the 13th century, it is believed that the ancient fort at Lo (Lo Manthang, Upper Mustang) was built to protect against the prolific Tamangs. The Ghorkas waged war on the Tamang heartland in the early to mid-1800s, and thus began a long history of suppression. The Newas and others engaged them as porters and low-level workers to enhance their own trade, which flourished. The Tamangs became the backbone of the trade, literally, as they hauled in the goods traded from China/Tibet.

Nowadays, Tamangs make up the majority of porters in the tourism industry and also number some fine Thangka painters and carpet weavers, but mostly they still remain uneducated agriculturists that have never reached the upper echelons of politics, military, or police.

Though through history's eyes they seem an oppressed race, if you meet a Tamang in person, which you more than likely will on this journey, they are proud and welcoming people known for their lively cultural dress, songs and dance.

Chepang

Along the Trans Nepal route, you will encounter the Chepang (also locally pronounced Chewang) people in the districts of Gorkha and Dhading, between Pokhara and Kathmandu. They are not solely a mid-hill people, however, with groups spreading down into the lower lands of mid-Nepal also.

The Chepangs are a rugged bunch and one of the poorest ethnic groups, with high illiteracy rates and insubstantial income. They practice both Hinduism and Buddhism.

They have clung to their identity and still kept many of their own ancient tribal rituals alive which are different from the traditional festivals of mainstream Hinduism.

Modern-day Chepangs have a more settled farming lifestyle in comparison to their semi-nomadic ancestors. Traditionally they were hunters, fishermen, and gatherers. The wild and rugged Mahtabharat (the Mid Hills) mountain ranges they call home make farming and stability difficult. Nowadays, development and deforestation have allowed them to farm maize, millet and bananas, leading to a more stable life. But modern life has had an impact on the nutrition and health of Chepangs. They once relied on a naturally foraged diet of yams, nuts, seeds, nettles and many wild varieties of food with high nutritional and medicinal value. The knowledge of which was passed down through generations. Now they have fallen in line with the modern concept that they must eat white rice, believing the misconception that it offers better nutritional values than their traditional diet.

Chepangs are easily recognizable by their shorter stature, Mongolian round faces and flat noses. They tend to live in huts made of wooden sticks and mud.

Sherpa

While Sherpas are perhaps the most well-known and romanticised ethnic group in Nepal, they comprise only 0.41% of the country's total population. While many think Sherpa is the name given to mountaineers or mountain porters, they are in fact one of Nepal's oldest ethnic groups. They hail from the mountainous regions in the east of Nepal, as their name suggests in Sherpa language Shar (East) and Pa (People). The group is of Tibetan ethnic origin and is predominantly Buddhist.

You will encounter sherpas as you pass below the Helambu and Solu Khumbu regions. An easily recognisable feature of Sherpa architecture are the gompas, distinctive religious sites where they practice daily rituals and traditions.

Historically a nomadic people that migrated down from the Tibetan Autonomous Region, they gained autonomy with Nepal in the 1400s when Nepal became a newly formed state. Nowadays, many sherpas have successfully moved into tourism-based business and gained fame as the unsung heroes of Chomolungma, the 'Mother of the World', or the mountain we all know as Mount Everest.

The Raute people.

Newars

The Newars comprise about half the population of the Kathmandu Valley. They form a linguistic and cultural community of primarily Indo-Aryan and Tibeto-Burman ethnicities following Hinduism and Buddhism, with Nepal Bhasa as their common language. Newars have developed a division of labour and a sophisticated urban civilisation not seen elsewhere in the Himalayan foothills. They are prolific artisans, especially in the areas of wood and brickwork. Their culture has been strongly influenced by Indian religious and social institutions and they celebrate an impressive number of festivals annually.

Raute

The Raute are the last nomadic people of Nepal and are extremely elusive, as they move location every four to five months and inhabit lands in the deeper areas of rural west Nepal. The latest census identified only 52 families (about 180 people) of these nomadic people left in Nepal. The Raute eat macaque monkey and langur as their staple, as well as foraging berries and nuts. Rautes emphasise that they wish to remain full-time foragers and not assimilate into the surrounding farming population.

The Mid West.

Route Overview

While Nepal is most famous for the High Himalayas, most of Nepal's cultural and ecological diversity are found in the hilly Mahabharat Mountain Range (commonly known as Nepal's Mid Hills), which range between 1000-3500m.

Occupying 68% of the country, these regions enjoy a temperate climate, and the land here is far more fertile than in the upper Himalayan region. At the high end, the Middle Hills range reaches an altitude of around 4000m above sea level.

The three lateral mountain sections of Nepal include the High Himalayas, the Middle Himalayas (the Mahābhārat mountain range) and the Lower Himalayas – the Churia Hills and The Terai. This trio of ranges span the country from West to East. Our trans-Nepal cycling journey traverses the Middle Himalayan range – the Mid Hills – and brushes the feet of the mighty High Himalayas across the country's length of approximately 1,650km.

We have chosen the Middle Himalayas route because it perfectly combines the physical challenge of uninterrupted cycling with adventure and rich cultural experiences throughout the full traverse of the country.

The High Himalayan route, following the mythical Great Himalayan Trail, is spectacular, but is not so suited for cycling – much of this route (over 50%) requires the rider to 'hike-a bike' (walk and push the bike) on many sections.

The third option is the flat Terai route along the fringes of the jungles to the south and the hot, sweaty cultural melting pot of the Indian border. This area is dominated by the East-West Highway – a busy road of high speed, heavy trucks and intensely polluting traffic. While flat and easy, the East-West Highway is not the safest, most desirable or the most challenging adventure that a lot of touring cyclists seek.

This brings us to our chosen route – following the 1,650km Mid Hills High Road. This ambitious road build, the longest of its kind in Nepal, began in 2008 and in true Nepali style is still, at the time of publication, incomplete. Here begins our trans-Nepal adventure, spanning from the far reaches of the wild and vastly unexplored west Nepal, through the more developed and culturally rich mid-region, right

Suspension bridge crossing,
Central Nepal.

into the rolling tea plantations of the East under the looming shadows of Mount Everest.

The Road should be fully paved in the coming five to seven years and will provide much-needed transport links for hundreds of rural communities to access the urban hubs of the country. However, due to the challenging profile of The Road and the rural areas it traverses, it is not expected to be busy with heavy traffic and commerce even when it is complete. Its main function will be to link mountainous mid-hill towns and communities, and not function as a transport vein for heavy goods, which will continue to use the Mahendra east-west highway that runs along the much flatter Terai region on the southern border with India.

In October 2023, The Road was approximately 60% paved, with the remaining 40% being mostly jeep tracks or newly carved rough road with gravel, good for both mountain bike and gravel bike. The full route can be completed in one single journey of approximately 26-30 days, or in multiple shorter journeys. Completing The Road in two stages is a good option, the first section being from the far-west to Pokhara (12-14 days) and the second, from Pokhara to the far-east (14-16 days).

The Road is 100% rideable and offers intrepid cyclists the opportunity to ride one of the most challenging cycling gauntlets on Earth – 1,650km across the Himalayas through one of the world's most remote and fascinating cultures.

The Far West.

Kathmandu

Few names tickle the imagination and evoke mystery and eastern romanticism like Kathmandu. Nestled in the sub-tropical Kathmandu Valley with soaring Himalayan peaks as a backdrop, this ancient city teems with life, chaos and spirituality.

Kathmandu is the perfect place for immersion and introduction into all things Nepali. After just a day of shuffling through the ramshackle streets and bulging shop fronts, absorbing the sights, sounds and smells, you will become quickly enchanted by the city and its melting pot of people, traditions and religions, from the predominant Hindu population to the Buddhist communities from Tibet and other Himalayan regions and the ancient culture of the Newar people.

The heart of the city, and focal point for most visitors is the old district of Thamel. To most, Thamel is a hectic yet positive immersion of the senses into Kathmandu life. It can be frantic and stressful, with a mind-boggling array of things to buy from shop fronts dripping with goods. Yet, a few steps off the main drag it is possible to find a quiet spot to relax and reflect, to close your eyes, breathe in the rich smells and aromas of this enchanting old city and enjoy a moment of serenity.

While it is certainly intense, you will feel generally comfortable and safe in Kathmandu if you keep your wits about you, especially in the more touristy parts of town. In Thamel you may be approached to buy a handmade instrument or some tiger balm, but if you're not interested, just smile and say no and the street hawkers will typically move on. There is generally very little insistence to buy goods on the streets.

Left: Durbar Square, the most famous and atmospheric place in Kathmandu.

Below: Phewa Lake and the town of Pokhara.

Pokhara

The beautiful lakeside town of Pokhara, Nepal's second city, is like a mini-Kathmandu along the fringes of Phewa Lake in central Nepal. The backdrop of the Annapurna Himalayas behind the lake makes for a stunning setting on a clear day.

As Pokhara is the jumping-off point to many treks and tours into the Annapurna Himalayas, there is a real sense of adventure and anticipation in the streets, all bulging with clothing and equipment to purchase for the adventure-bound intrepid traveller. As Pokhara is also the end point of many trips and tours, there are many good restaurants and bars to relax in after a gruelling trip, where travellers can truly kick back, rest, recuperate and celebrate.

Central Nepal.

PART 2
Preparing For
Your Trip

NEPAL'S SEASONS
Choosing When to Go

Nepal has vastly varying climates, both regionally and from season to season.

Nepal uniquely boasts six seasons, so consider these when planning your journey. Average temperatures are given for the altitude range 1,800m to 3,000m.

Basanta Ritu (Spring): Mid-March to Mid-May

Average daytime temperature: 21°C

Average nighttime temperature: 11°C

Chance of rain: 16%

Early summer is the recommended time to attempt The Road – temperatures begin to increase, and the weather remains stable, the clear skies juxtaposed against the blooming spring Himalayan flora. There are also a number of spring festivals to enjoy, including Holi in March and Nepalese New Year in April.

Left: Central Nepal.

Grishma Ritu (Summer): Mid-May to Mid-July

Average daytime temperature: 26°C

Average nighttime temperature: 12°C

Chance of rain: 32%

Temperatures, humidity and rainfall steadily increase through this season, making it more of a challenge than early summer.

Varsha Ritu (Rainy): Mid-July to Mid-September

Average daytime temperature: 27°C with humidity

Average nighttime temperature: 14°C

Chance of rain: 63%

While this is one of the most dramatic and beautiful times in Nepal, it is possibly the worst time to travel. The monsoon hits Nepal's Mid Hills with a vengeance. Roads become slick with mud, landslides become a real danger and it's swelteringly hot and humid. The upside is the lush green fields and mystical, cloud-draped mountain views.

Sharad Ritu (Autumn):
Mid-September to Mid-November

Average daytime temperature: 24°C

Average nighttime temperature: 12°C

Chance of rain: 17%

The later you get into this season, the drier and colder the weather becomes. The skies are generally clear with great views. The days are warm and sunny enough for T-shirts. During Sharad, a lot of Nepal's main festivals like Dashian and Tihar happen, which coincide with the end of the Summer Harvest. This is a great time to travel and cycle. It is also peak trekking season, so Kathmandu and Pokhara are bustling and the hiking trails are busy.

Hemanta Ritu (Pre-winter):
Mid-November to Mid-January

Average daytime temperature: 18°C

Average nighttime temperature: 3°C

Chance of rain: 3%

The Road can be attempted in late autumn with the right kit and planning, but it is cold, so be prepared to encounter some snow in the higher elevations.

Shishir Ritu (Winter):
Mid-January to Mid-March

Average daytime temperature: 21°C

Average nighttime temperature: 5°C

Chance of rain: 6%

January and February are also cold and you will likely encounter snow at higher altitudes, but skies are clear. With the right clothing and equipment, The Road can be attempted in these months. As March approaches, temperatures warm quickly.

Left: Getting some shade, the Mid-West.

What Kit to Bring

It is easy to get carried away and pack excessive amounts, but it's sensible to travel light, with the correct (minimal) amount of gear, for a comfortable trip.

Don't forget, most airlines only allow 25kg of luggage (+7kg of hand luggage), so if you are bringing your own bike, you have some tough decisions to make in terms of what you bring and what you leave behind. What follows is a list of the recommended minimum kit and equipment required for travel during the recommended seasons of spring and autumn. Please note, this list is a recommended list for riders using jeep support. If you are bike-packing you will have to narrow this list down a lot more, depending on the capacity of your paniers.

For riding

2 bib shorts

1 lightweight sport short with pockets

2 tech T-shirts (long sleeve recommended for sun protection)

2 pairs socks

1 buff

1 thin fleece

1 wind shell jacket

2 cycling gloves (1 covered fingers)

1 bike helmet

Day backpack

Basic first aid kit (for cuts and grazes)

Hand sanitiser

Sunglasses

Sunscreen

Inner tube, levers, pump, chain tool, chain lube

Energy snacks

For downtime

1 warm trousers

1 warm fleece

2 T-shirts

2 underwear

2 socks

1 towel

1 beanie

1 gloves

Accessories

Head torch

Washing line

Toiletries bag with additional first aid

Extensive bike tool kit, including extra chain and tyre

Nutrition Along The Road

We are all different when it comes to nutritional planning for endurance events. Some like to consume just natural food for their energy, some like to follow the science with high-impact manufactured energy foods and some like a balance of the two. I am not a nutritionist or a food science expert, but I can share my experiences from having done many long-distance, multi-day mountain bike trips.

During our traverse of The Road I decided to go au naturel with my nutrition for the full duration. I have often carried energy bars and gels (which are collectively heavy) and have mostly gone home with them unused. For me, they've just not been needed. With careful planning and stocking, all the nutrition you need is available along The Road.

Here is a typical daily food and drink consumption intake for long days on the bike on The Road. These foods are available along the route in most settlements, except for chocolate. It's best to stock up in Kathmandu with a few boxes of Snickers or Mars bars.

Breakfast

Scrambled eggs with chilli and onion

2 roti/chapati

Black coffee

Water

Mid-morning snack

Black tea

Fruit – bananas, apple, pomegranate

Chocolate

Water

Lunch

Veg noodle soup with egg

Fruit – bananas, apples

Snacks – moong dal, masala chips

Water

Sugary soft drink

Mid-afternoon snack

Black tea

Fruit – bananas, apple, pomegranate

Chocolate

Biscuits

Water

Sugary soft drink

On arrival at destination

It is highly recommended to eat scrambled eggs within 45 minutes of arrival to absorb protein into the body after a long day.

Dinner

Dal bhat

1L water

1-2 beers

Above: Roadside snacks.

Right: Fried noodles.

Out on The Road.

Which Bike for The Road?

Much to our surprise, The Road turned out to be relatively smooth going on jeep tracks and paved for most of the way, so any type of quality bike would probably make it.

There are a number of stony sections along the way, but they only last for a few hundred metres, and bikes can be carried as quickly as they can be ridden on most of these more technical sections.

Here are four bike recommendations:

1. **Cross-country (XC) full-suspension mountain bike (most recommended).** These lightweight bikes with full suspension allow a high degree of comfort and flexibility in all terrain. With a dropper seat-post and suspension that can lock, it's a no-brainer that the XC full-suspension bike is the dream machine for The Road. Semi-slick tires recommended.

2. Hardtail MTB – Perfectly fine for the trip. Good for climbing and absorbent of shocks on the descents. However, given the distances covered and the length of some of the bumpy descents, an investment in a full-suspension XC bike is recommended, but not essential. Semi-slick tires are recommended.

3. Gravel bike – The Road can be tackled on a gravel bike without too many concerns. There are some rough sections that many need carrying over, but experienced gravel riders will be able to ride just about 100% of the way.

4. E-mountain bike – At the time of publication, The Road, in its entirety, has never been tackled on an e-bike, but from our research and reconnaissance trip we found no shortage of electricity at all stops along the way. We met a group of e-bikers riding a multi-day trip from Kathmandu to Pokhara along the route and they had no problems at all with charging. Just note that there are numerous sections along The Road, particularly in the far west and far east, where there are no settlements for up to 30km, so, if you are up for the e-bike challenge, always make sure you are fully charged before you set off each morning.

If you take a risk and run out of juice, The Road is not forgiving for pushing 25kg+ of metal up and over its endless hills. E-bikes can be rented through Himalayan Single Track bike shop in Kathmandu.

Hybrid option – A hardtail mountain bike with fitted drop handlebars could be a great DIY hybrid option. This would give you comfort as well as flexible options for your hands during the long days.

There are a number of stony sections along the way, but they only last for a few hundred metres.

Below: Suspension bridge, the Mid-West.

Technical and Endurance Levels

In the guide section (Part 3) of the book there is a 1 to 5 scale for the technical and endurance levels of riding each day. Here is a guide to those levels:

Technical Level:

1. Easy: Paved road.

2. Easy Overall: Paved with some broken road and potholes.

3. Moderate: Paved road and jeep tracks, some bumpy sections.

4. Challenging: Overall poor-quality paved road and jeep tracks, sand on sections, mostly bumpy.

5. Difficult: Poor quality roads, technical sections, sand on sections.

Endurance Level:

1. Easy: short distance, minimal climbing.

2. Easy overall: short distance, a small number of climbs.

3. Moderate: mid-level distance, some reasonable climbs (up to 500m ascent).

4. Challenging: long distance, numerous long climbs +500m, difficult surface sections.

5. Difficult: long distance, numerous long climbs +750m, long steep gradients (+15%) difficult surface sections.

In summary, The Road can be ridden on a hardtail mountain bike or a gravel bike. It's certainly not challenging terrain for technical mountain bikers, but a long-distance 'Grand Tour' of gruelling endurance through some of the most remote mountainous areas of Asia.

Don't be put off by the technical levels, it really is not a technical challenge, but you do need stamina, courage, dogged determination and an open mind if you want to pedal 1650km across the Nepal Himalayas.

You do need stamina, courage, dogged determination and an open mind if you want to pedal 1650km across the Nepal Himalayas.

Training for The Road

This is a tricky one, as everyone has their own goals, pace, methods, philosophies, gym coach or fit-friend-advisory-service, so I'll keep this brief and just share my advice on how we made it across The Road in a reasonable time (29 days). I travelled with my friend and route cartographer, Mark, who was sixty when we completed the challenge together (which was, in fact, the recce for this book). We stopped regularly to take notes, photos and co-ordinates, with regular tea stops to consolidate info and data.

Physical Preparation

From a reasonable baseline of fitness (able to comfortably climb 500m on a bike), work up to climbing 1500m in three back-to-back days one week prior to departure to Nepal. That's the minimum – simple as that. This level of fitness will take approximately three months from base fitness if you can train two to three times per week. Multi-day long-distance rides with lots of climbing will always be the best preparation for the trip, as that's what you'll be doing on The Road. The fitter you are, the more enjoyable the experience will be.

High-intensity training sessions once a week, then twice or three times a week closer to departure, are a big boost to fitness and recovery. These can be done on a turbo trainer or gym bike, taking 30 minutes per session – a five-minute warm up followed by intense intervals with resistance for twenty minutes until you're soaking wet, your legs are throbbing, and your heart is bursting out of your chest, then a five-minute warm down and stretching. There are many options online if you cannot conjure up your own.

Do some all-round body weights to ensure your body is as strong and balanced as possible to reduce the risk of injuries, particularly in the lower back region. Enhancing core stability (planks, sit ups, crunchies) and leg strength (squats, lunges, leg presses) is key to ensuring a well-conditioned body for the gruelling challenge of The Road. And having the ability to run at least 5km comfortably would be beneficial for overall fitness. Training runs should include some jogging up long stairs or steps.

It's also advisable to do some hiking on steep ascent terrain (or walking up high-rise block floors) in the weeks prior to departure as some sections of The Road can be very

steep (15%+) and you will be almost as fast and expend far less energy by walking your bike on these steep sections.

Mental Preparation

The Riding

If this is your first trip to a developing country, your mind can get carried away with the potential risks and dangers you perceive there to be in a country like Nepal. These fears and apprehensions are rational fear-of-the-unknown thoughts. But as we generally learn through experience, most of the things we fear rarely manifest into reality, and the risks of cycling in Nepal are not really higher than cycling in any developed country. The riding along The Road is non-technical and for the most part remote, so you rarely encounter heavy traffic or potential danger. Only in and around Kathmandu and Pokhara will you have to navigate in traffic, which can be a lot of fun if you have your wits about you.

The dangers arise from riding without caution – hurtling recklessly down long descents with sand on the road, overtaking trucks without knowing the road ahead or going off-piste and attempting jumps in unknown terrain.

The Road is a marathon, not a sprint, and self-preservation is the key to making it in one piece. Ride safely. Still enjoy the thrilling descents, pop some air when you see a lip on the side of the road, enjoy overtaking a truck when the road is clear, but don't take risks that could jeopardise your safety and your quest to complete The Road.

The Mindset

Arrive with an open, patient mind. Schedules will be delayed, things may break down, plans may have to be adapted if situations arise. But things always work themselves out in Nepal. The Nepalis are the most enterprising people you could ever hope to meet, and they find a solution for everything. Just go with it, never get angry, put your trust in the local people and there is always a way. You will have the time of your life. Prepare yourself for that as well, and don't just focus on the potential negatives.

The Road is a marathon, not a sprint, and self-preservation is the key to making it in one piece.

Getting to Nepal

Flights from the UK and Europe

There are a number of options, but there are no direct flights to Kathmandu from Europe, so at least one stop is required en route. Recommended airlines include Qatar, Emirates, Etihad and Air India, all of which provide just one stopover. Travel time can be expected to be 16-20 hours each way.

Fares are seasonal, so expect to pay 900-1400 USD for return flights in the spring and autumn months and 600-900 USD in the summer (monsoon) months.

Flights from North America

If you live on the east coast of North America it is faster to fly to Nepal via Europe and then the Middle East or India. From the west coast it is recommended to go in the opposite direction via the Far East. Recommended airlines for this Eastern route include Cathay Pacific, Thai Airways and Singapore Airlines. Travelling to Kathmandu can be expected to be 20-30 hours each way.

Flight prices vary due to no alignment of seasons, so prices for return flights can range from 1000-2500 USD.

Flights from Australia, New Zealand and South Africa

Flying to Nepal from Australia or New Zealand requires transit through Asia or the Middle East. Due to the long distances, two or more stopovers may be required. Recommended airlines include Singapore Airlines, Thai Airways, Cathay Pacific, Malaysian Airlines, Qatar and Emirates.

One option worth considering for time and cost savings with the Asian carriers is flying in and out of Delhi and picking up an Indian budget airline flight to Kathmandu (e.g. Spicejet, Indigo, Vistara).

At the time of publication, return flights to Kathmandu from Australia and New Zealand range from 1500-2500 USD, with travel times of 22-30 hours each way.

From South Africa there are regular flights from Johannesburg to Kathmandu via the Middle East (Emirates and Qatar) and Singapore (Singapore Airlines). A further option is to travel via India, where you can pick up a budget flight into Kathmandu.

At the time of publication, fares range from 1000-2000 USD return to Kathmandu from South Africa, with travel times of 15-25 hours each way.

Visas

For many nationalities, Nepal will issue 'On Arrival' Tourist visas that follow a quick and simple procedure on arrival at immigration. At Tribhuvan International Airport (Kathmandu) you may experience some queues for the visa during peak tourist season. If you wish to avoid the queues, you can also obtain a visa from Nepalese diplomatic missions stationed abroad prior to your arrival. Likewise, other entry and exit points at land border regions also provide 'On Arrival' visas to foreign nationals entering Nepal via land.

While you can use different modes of payment to pay for your visa, it is advisable to carry some cash to be on the safe side.

On Arrival Visa Fees (July 2023)

15 Days – 30 USD
30 Days – 50 USD
90 Days – 125 USD

For an up-to-date list of nationalities eligible for a visa on arrival, and more comprehensive visa information, visit the Nepal government's immigration/visa webpages.

Arrival by Land

If you are crossing into Nepal by land from India, be sure you are entering through a border that is open to foreign travellers, as not all of them are. At the time of publication, Jhulaghat border in the west and Chiyo Banjyang border in the east do not permit foreign travellers to enter Nepal.

Expenses

Nepal is not an expensive country. If you choose to travel independently and live simply, you could budget around 2,500 NPR (20 USD) per day for food and lodgings while you are on The Road. In Kathmandu and Pokhara you will need more, around 4000 NPR (30 USD) per day if you are happy with a comfortable, but basic hotel in Thamel. Things get expensive when you start buying beers or alcohol. One beer will set you back around 600NRP in any part of the country. Public transport is cheap as is access to historical sites and monuments.

If you choose to go with a tour company, they will send you an offer for the entire trip, which will include jeep travel to the starting point, jeep support for the duration of the trip and a ride back to Kathmandu from the end point. You will also have an experienced guide who will ride with you. Included in the offer will be all accommodation and three meals per day.

The only company currently offering The Road packages is Himalayan Single Track in Satghumti, Thamel, Kathmandu.

Health and Safety

Health

Check with your government's health advice on what vaccinations are needed for your trip to Nepal. Government health sites will also be up to date if there are any flare ups of diseases (e.g. dengue, malaria) in certain areas of the country. But overall, on The Road you will be riding in Nepal's temperate and subalpine zones, so the standard vaccinations for overseas travel will generally be sufficient if you travel during the recommended seasons (spring and autumn).

Health services outside the Kathmandu valley and Pokhara are sparse, so it is recommended to carry a full medical kit for accidents, and for infections. This should include a course of antibiotics for infected wounds and a course for parasite infections.

If you travel as recommended – with a guide and a support vehicle – you can be safely evacuated to a regional hospital within two to eight hours at any point on The Road. With vehicle support, you have much less to worry about than if you are riding independently. If you are bike-packing without a guide or support, you should ensure you have a comprehensive medical kit, know how to use it all and possibly know in advance where the nearest hospitals are located along each section of The Road.

It is also important that you ensure you have appropriate travel insurance for unexpected medical evacuation or local treatment.

In terms of personal health, it is important to be mindful of what you eat and drink. Most illnesses along The Road will likely be parasites coming into contact with dirty water. With food, make sure hot foods are cooked properly, especially meats. Try to ascertain if meat is fresh before it is cooked. If you drink hot drinks in rural areas make sure the water has been boiled properly. Wash fruits well and try to stick to fruits that you have to peel/open yourself, like bananas, oranges and pomegranates. Try to avoid foods that have been pre-peeled or rinsed in local untreated water (salad, peeled apples etc). If you want a peeled apple, do it yourself and rinse with bottled or boiled water. Also make sure plates and cutlery are clean. And of course, drink only boiled or bottled cold water. If a new water bottle cap seal is broken, it's safest to exchange for a correctly sealed bottle, or discard it for a new one. But given the significant problem of plastic pollution in Nepal, it is recommended to use water purification and filtration methods (tablets, filters, boiling) as much as you can to avoid adding to the plastic problem.

For personal hygiene, wash your hands regularly in settlements, especially before eating, and it's advisable to always carry hand sanitiser during the trip. Also, clean your teeth with bottled or boiled water, especially in remote regions.

Personal Safety

Nepal is, overall, a safe country for foreigners to travel freely. Nepalis are some of the most hospitable people you will ever meet, and they treat visitors with respect and gratitude. That said, you should still take standard precautions. Pickpockets exist in Kathmandu and to a lesser extent Pokhara, and it's advisable not to walk around late at night alone in urban areas. The biggest threat to personal safety, from our experience on The Road, is encountering drunk people, especially around festival time, when drinking can go to the next level. Most locals in the countryside are happy drinkers and some wonderful conversations can be had in the wee hours, but we did experience one or two unhappy drunks along The Road late in the

evenings, which could feel quite intimidating if you are alone or in a small group. The nuisance, however, is no different from what we could experience in any of our hometowns on a Saturday night.

Road Travel

The thought of travelling on Himalayan roads fills many people's minds with terror, and these concerns are sometimes warranted. Road travel can be hair-raising, and accidents are frequent in Nepal. To put yourself at ease, travel with a reputable company and you will be in safe hands, travelling in modern jeeps with drivers well used to western sensitivities. If you feel your driver is not driving safely, just tell him/her and they will drive more cautiously. You also have to become accustomed to the dramatic scenery around you as you travel by road in Nepal. It's all part of the experience!

As you are cycling across the entire country, your only need for transport is to the start line in Dadeldhura and from the finish line in Bhadrapur. Both points are accessible by low-altitude paved highways, which are relatively safe compared to the higher mountain roads.

Ethics and Fitting In

Fitting in is relatively easy in Nepal if you follow a few simple guidelines and respect some cultural nuances.

Learning to speak a bit of the language, dressing conservatively and showing some interest in the local culture will go a long way.

Be sensitive when it comes to your clothing. While nowadays it's acceptable to wear whatever in cities and tourist areas, rural Nepalis are not used to seeing skimpily clad people, so it's better to dress in shirts and decent shorts or long pants when in rural areas.

Be a bit considerate around temples. Ask if it's okay to go inside and take notice of what others are doing – if they are taking their shoes off, take your shoes off. The normal direction to walk around a temple is clockwise. Also, some temples do not allow foreigners into the inner sanctum, so always ask first before you enter and ask for permission to take any photos.

An easy way to engage with locals is to let them try your bike or show them your photos and videos – they will love this, especially the kids.

Rural Nepalis generally live as family groups and they find it curious when people travel alone, especially females, and they will ask a lot of questions about you.

Don't get offended when people comment on or ask about:

• Your marital status.
• Ethnic/religious origins.
• Your weight.

These types of questions are quite normal in Nepal and are asked out of a sense of genuine curiosity. A lot of people will also be interested in which country you come from, mostly because they might have family living overseas. These are normal conversation starters.

On some occasions, questions can be aggressive due to the consumption of alcohol. If you feel harassed, just walk away or go to your room and ask for some privacy.

Public affection is not really shown in Nepal. It can be considered awkward to kiss or hold hands in public. (But it's normal for same-sex friends to hold hands and hug each other.)

Eating etiquette – Nepalese people eat with their hands. Hand washing is normal and expected both before and after meals. There will always be a place to wash, just ask. Nepalis eat with their right hand only – the

left hand is considered polluted, as that is what is used for washing after going to the toilet.

It is also more polite to give and receive things with your right hand i.e. food items, money and gifts.

Photography – Before clicking and posting photos, you should consider that maybe that charactered face of a wrinkled old man or the cute rosy cheeks of a baby might not want to be shown to the world via your Instagram account or Vlogg.

You should always ask first before taking photos and respect people's privacy.

Feet – Touching other people or pointing at things with your feet is considered rude. If somebody accidentally touches you with their foot, they will make amends by touching their hand to the foot and forehead. This is common.

Above: The ladies of Dailekh District.

Shoes – Always remove your shoes when entering a house. A lot of places will have a set of slippers as well, and bathrooms will also have a set of slippers outside. These bathroom slippers are just for use in the bathroom, not other places in the house.

Using the toilet – Most households will have a toilet either attached to the house or a short distance away. First check if there is water, most will have a bucket/jug. If not, ask. Nepalis use water to wash themselves, they do not use toilet paper. You can carry your own. It's okay, if there is a bin, put the paper there rather than flush it. The water is used to both clean your private bits and to flush the toilet. Some toilets are cleaner than others!

Women's hygiene – NEVER flush your pads/tampons in the toilet, as the plumbing in Nepal is not the best. Just wrap it and carry it out with you until you find a place to get rid of it.

In some village cultures menstruating women are isolated and not allowed in kitchens, temples and other places. While we do not condone this, it is a good idea to be discrete about it should you be menstruating.

It is recommended that travelling women use a menstrual cup as it's easy to use, hygienic and a non-waste product. Tampons will not be available in most rural areas, at the very least you will be able to buy some form of pads only. It's best to carry your own.

Giving way on the trail – When riding your bike, should you venture off road onto walking trails or into temple/village areas, remember these are the walking ways of the local people, always give way to them.

Should you see people approaching with livestock, give them some space and try not to startle the animals, it's also always a good idea to ride slowly in village areas.

Dogs along The Road – Dogs can aggressively chase cyclists when you cross their area or territory. This is purely an instinct nine times out of ten. If you simply slow down, make eye contact with the dog and pass slowly, they will turn away and ignore you. All the dog is doing is guarding its territory. Dogs will be twice as aggressive when caged or tied, so don't approach them.

Should you see people approaching with livestock, give them some space and try not to startle the animals.

Language

Nepalese people are super appreciative of people who try to speak their language. It's a shortcut to making friends here and many villages will be fascinated by you. In a lot of the more remote areas also, English is not well spoken and a basic handle on some keywords can help you immensely to get what you need.

Do note that in remote areas, Nepalese is not always the first language. There are many ethnic languages and some of the older generation may not have a strong grasp of Nepali.

Namaste – Hello (literally means 'I salute the God in you').

Namaskar – Hello (formal).

Both are also used as goodbye.

Most locals do not use the above-mentioned phrases in day-to-day life. A typical rural greeting is more like the below (depending on the time of day).

Chai khahnu bhayo? – Have you drank tea?

Khana khahnu bhayo? – Have you had your dal bhat?

Khaja Khahnu bhayo? – Have you had your snacks?

These phrases are a simplistic and delightful insight into how rural people care that you are well fed, as being fed and healthy is the ultimate sign of wellbeing.

Common Courtesies

Many people ask how to say please and thank you in Nepali. Nepali is a practical language and these words are not often used.

Dhanyabad – Thank you.

Kripieya – Please (very formal).

Swagatham – You're welcome.

Politeness is normally expressed in the way things are said, for example:

Dinu – 'Give' is the direct verb and would be used for children or close friends.

Dinus – More polite: 'Please give it to me.'

Harju lia dinus – High respect, asking for something from elders and people above you in status.

In most cases the simple addition of 'nus' to a verb will imply politeness.

Linus – Please take it / **Linu** – Take.

Basnus – Please sit down / **Basnu** – Sit down / **Bas** – Sit (stern, as spoken to children).

Aunus – Please come / **Aunu** – Come.

Jannus – Please go or leave / **Janu** – To go / **Jau** – Go (in a rude way).

Food Basics

Chow chow anda – Noodles and egg, normally soup style.

Dal bhat – The national dish of Nepal. Rice and lentils served with some form of vegetable curry and pickles.

Khana – Food, normally refers to Dal Bhat.

Masu – Meat / **Dal bhat masu** – Dal bhat with meat curry.

Achara – Pickle.

Tarakari – Vegetable curry.

Kukhura – Chicken / **Kukhura ko masu** – Chicken meat.

Bhakra – Goat / **Bhakra ko masu** – goat meat

Macha – Fish / **Macha ko masu** – Fish Meat

Bhainsi – Buffalo / **Bhainsi ko masu** – Buffalo meat (also referred to as buff).

Anda – Eggs / **Umaleko anda** – Boiled egg.

Kera – Banana.

Mewa – Papaya.

Suntala – Local orange.

Most other fruits will be referred to by the English name.

Pani – Water / **Khanepani** – Drinking water.

Chai – Tea / **Dudha chai** – Milk tea / **Khalo chia** – Black tea / **Kagati chia** – Lemon tea (all will have sugar).

*Note – Coffee is not a staple in rural areas. You may find Nescafé, but if you're a coffee addict then buy some local beans in Kathmandu or Pokhara and make your own coffee.

Local Booze

Raksi – A spirit not dissimilar to Sake. Can be made from rice, millet or buckwheat. Varies in strength from household to household. Drink with care! Raksi can be served at room temperature or heated up on a cold winter night.

Chang – Referred to as local beer, this is a thick drink which is a by-product of corn or rice harvest. It can be sour or sweet and is normally served cold on hot days. In some remote areas a bowl of thick corn chang is considered a meal. Less alcoholic than raksi.

Tongba – Hot beer, normally found in higher colder regions in winter. A specialty of the Sherpa and Tamang people. It is fermented millet which is served in a special bamboo or metal cup. Hot water is poured over it and it is sucked

The Far West.

through a filtering straw. The water can be topped up several times. It is a warming drink. You don't always notice the alcohol effect until you stand up!

Customising Your Food

Nepalis love sugar, salt and spice and most regional areas will not automatically regulate it for travellers like they do in tourist restaurants. Many Nepalese people, especially in village areas, feel that salt gives you power and energy to work and they feel weak without it. The same goes for spice.

Here are a few phrases to help regulate Nepali condiments!

Chini – Sugar / **Ghulio** – Sweet / **Chini Kam** – Less sugar.

Khursani – Chilli / **Piro** – Spicy / **Piro kam** – Less spicy.

Nun – Salt / **Nunilo** – Salty / **Nunilo chha** – It's salty / **Nun kam** – Less salty.

Thorai – A small amount.

Ali ali – A little bit / **'Ali ali nun rakhnuhos'** – 'Please add only a little salt'.

Dherai – A lot (a large amount).

The Far West.

Tato – Hot (as in temperature/related to food or liquid) / **Garmi** – It's hot (as in weather or feeling).

Chiso – Cold (as in temperature/related to food or liquid) / **Jhando** – Cold (as in weather or feeling).

Khanekura key cha? – What is there to eat?

Bhayo – It's enough, or I'm full.

Mitho cha – It was tasty/delicious.

Handy Words and Phrases

Kati ho? How much is it?

Ho – Yes / **Hoina** – No (general terms).

Sutne taou chaa? Is there a place to sleep?

Milchaa? – Is it possible?

Hola – Maybe/possibly.

Photo khicnu huncha? Can I take your photo? (Polite form.)

Thik cha? – Is everything OK?/ Are you OK? (Casual form.)

Thik cha – I'm OK or it's OK (casual form.)

Ma – Me.

Mero – Mine or my.

Tapai – You.

Tapai ko – Yours.

Mero nam ...... ho – My name is ......

Tapai ko nam ke ho? – What is your name?

Bhok lagyo – I'm hungry.

Thakai lagyo – I'm tired.

Ma haraye – I'm lost.

Ma birami chu – I'm sick.

Sahayog garnus – Please help.

Directions

Bato – Road.

Bato chha? – Is there a road?

Toilet kaha chha? – Where is the toilet?

Khanekura khahaa paincha? – Where can we get food?

Khahaa jancha? – Where are you going?

Khato ho? – Where is it?

Bhaiya – Left.

Daiya – Right.

Sidha – Straight.

Ukalo – Uphill.

Urallo – Downhill.

Ghado – Hard.

Sajilo – Easy.

Taadha – Far.

Najik – Close.

Some Typical Nepali Expressions

Nepalis have some wonderful expressions that are used every day:

Tei ta – Oh well! (Oh well, that happened, let's move on.)

Ek chin – Literal meaning is 'in one moment', but can mean anything from 'in a moment' to 'in a few hours', or possibly never.

Este ho – 'That's just the way it is' – one of the most popular terms used as an explanation to why something is, or is not, working or functioning, used in all situations as we would use a shrug of the shoulders.

Ke garne? – What can we do? (Shit happens.)

PART 3
The Route and
Guidebook

The Route and Guidebook

This is not a comprehensive guidebook detailing all places of interest, accommodation and eateries. Its objective is to provide the reader with enough information to create a spark of motivation to undertake this once-in-a-lifetime challenge with an intrepid spirit, and to use this book as your rough guide. Every adventure tends to write itself as it unfolds, and I hope these pages will act as a catalyst to your curiosity of cycling through the Himalayas and set you off on your own journey of discovery.

Important, please read...

The following section includes the route data for completing The Road and all key information, such as recommended accommodation and daily route info. During our research and reconnaissance trip we used digital mapping through three sources, namely Google Maps, Strava and Garmin, and the information in this guide is a consolidation of these sources. Given the remoteness of parts of The Road, there were often inconsistencies in distances and altitudes between sources, so please note this and be aware that you will likely have small variations in your results as well. You will also come across settlements that are not listed on Google Maps or Google Earth, and there will also be settlements listed on Google Maps and Google Earth that sometimes do not seem to exist as you ride through them. This is when you know you're well and truly in rural and remote Nepal.

We have done our best to be comprehensive and to consolidate data and route information where possible, but please be very much aware that this is a rough guide to crossing the Middle Himalayas. If you're travelling independently without a guide and support vehicle, it's highly advisable to bring basic camping equipment – a tent and sleeping bag, just in case you don't have the energy to make it to the destination on some of the long days. If you decide to camp, it's recommended to do so in, or next to settlements, where locals will always be welcoming and will often offer to provide you with a meal, and possibly a bed.

As explained earlier in the book, The Road follows the route of the government's official Mid Hills High Road, so it's difficult to go off course. However, there are some places along the way where you may encounter other small road options. In such cases, if you are not quite sure of the way, always stop and ask a local if you are going in the right direction to your destination for that day.

But don't let this small level of uncertainty put you off, you are unlikely to get lost. While The Road is mostly remote, there is life and human activity all the way along it, since it loosely follows an ancient trading route that still links communities today. And as the paved road develops, further life and activity will develop.

Because of these potential uncertainties in this quite uncharted part of Nepal, and because of the amount of kit and resources you will need for each leg of the trip, it is highly recommended to travel with a tour company and a professional guide with local experience and a support vehicle (which can follow you along the entire route). This will allow you to ride freely and quickly, safe in the knowledge you are in good hands. In the unlikely event of something going wrong, you can be swiftly evacuated to safety.

At the time of publication, the only tour company offering The Road – fully guided and supported packages, is Himalayan Single Track (HST) in Thamel, Kathmandu. HST provided the guide and support for our research and reconnaissance trip for this book, so they know the route well.

Whichever way you choose to take on The Road, it will be an adventure.

It is highly recommended to travel with a tour company and a professional guide with local experience and a support vehicle. This will allow you to ride freely and quickly, safe in the knowledge you are in good hands.

The Start Line
Far Western Province

Dadeldhura

The Road begins in the Far West region of Nepal, close to the Indian border at the town of Dadeldhura.

Dadeldhura is a district with a hill town of the same name. The town is surrounded by dense forest and mountains, with a heritage of rich cultural and traditional diversity. As the most developed district of the Far West hill regions, Dadeldhura is a good place to stock up on supplies before rolling your wheels to the start line of The Road.

Getting to Dadeldhura

From Kathmandu by land

Private jeep – In a private jeep the drive from Kathmandu is approximately 22 hours. Many travel agencies in the streets of Thamel can organise jeep transfers. Costs per day for a private jeep and a driver range from 90-150 USD.

Bus – From Kathmandu to Dhangadhi by bus takes 18-20 hours. Private companies offering this service include Yatra Nepal and Vivaan Adventure (Approx. 2700 NPR one way). You then need to take another bus (local) to Dadeldhura (5.5hrs, 500 NPR + 200 NPR per bike).

From Kathmandu by air and bus

If you have a guide and support vehicle carrying your bikes and you don't fancy the 22-hour jeep ride from Kathmandu, you can fly to Dhangadhi and arrange to meet your jeep at Dhangadhi airport for the ride to Dadeldhura (4.5hrs).

Kathmandu to Dhangadhi flight, 55 mins (190 USD one way). Options: Shree Air, Buddha Air, Yeti Air.

If you are travelling independently, after the flight you can take the public bus from Dhangadhi to Dadeldhura (5.5hrs, 500 NPR + 200 NPR per bike).

From Pokhara by bus

Pokhara to Dhangadhi by bus takes around 20 hours. This can be arranged through travel agents on the streets of Pokhara, who use various private bus companies. You will then need to take the public bus from Dhangadhi to Dadeldhura (5.5hrs, 500 NPR + 200 NPR per bike). There are no flight options at the time of writing.

The Far West.

Recommended Place to Stay in Dadeldhura

Hotel: Rato Gurans Resort.

Room rate: 2200 NPR per night (twin share).

Meal prices: 500 NPR (dal bhat).

The Far West.

THE ROAD SECTION 1
Dadeldhura – Pokhara
Days 1-13

Days 1-13
Dadeldhura – Pokhara

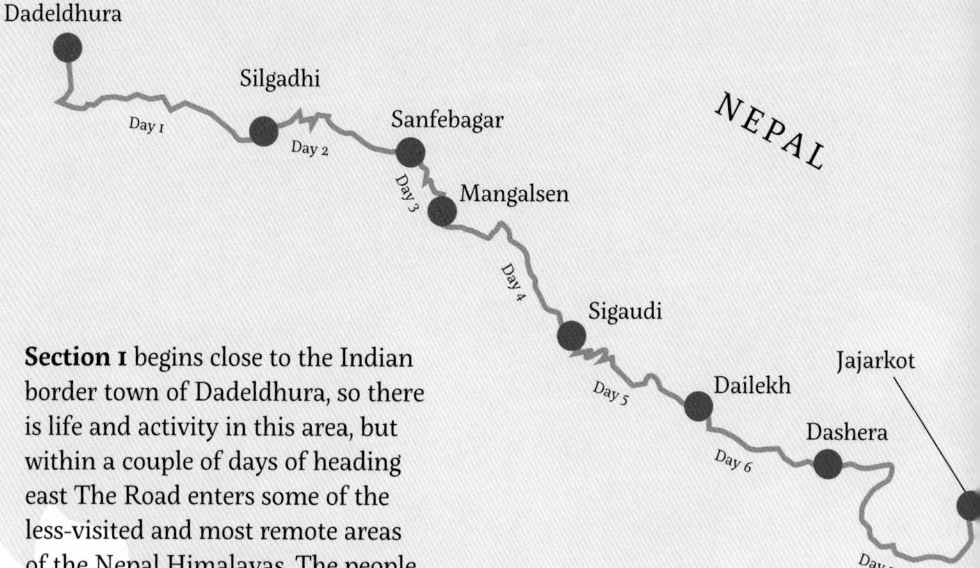

Dadeldhura

Silgadhi

Sanfebagar

Day 1

Day 2

Mangalsen

Day 3

NEPAL

Day 4

Sigaudi

Jajarkot

Day 5

Dailekh

Dashera

Day 6

Day 7

Section 1 begins close to the Indian border town of Dadeldhura, so there is life and activity in this area, but within a couple of days of heading east The Road enters some of the less-visited and most remote areas of the Nepal Himalayas. The people of the far west are poor, but rich in spirit. They are curious of western travellers, but quickly engage, and wonder why on Earth you are on bikes when you can afford to buy a car or take a bus. Along the way you will cross through communities of Dalit people – the 'untouchables' – the lowest caste of people in Nepal, who are born into a continual cycle of poverty, forbidden to improve their social status.

NEPAL

These are some of the kindest and most generous people you will ever meet. If you are lucky, you may also encounter the Raute people, the last nomadic people of Nepal who live only in the depths of western Nepal and live on a staple diet of monkeys and lemurs. The Road along Section I is mostly paved, with numerous unpaved broken sections that are not too difficult to traverse.

The climbs are long and intense, and the descents will blow your mind. As you approach Pokhara, civilisation returns, along with noise, dust, pollution and blaring horns. It is here you will view the high Himalayas for the first time, a moment you will never forget.

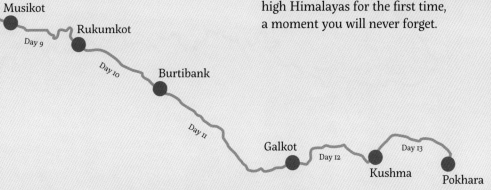

The complete GPX files for the entire route are available for free to all those who buy the book. Recommended for use with Strava, Garmin or similar reputable digital mapping applications.

Day 1: Dadeldhura – Silghadi

Distance: 72km

Cycling Time: 5hrs

Climbing: 1224m

Technical Level: 1/5

Endurance Level: 4/5

Route Summary

Starting at Ugratara Temple, this fully paved route begins with a 5km climb, followed by a fast and sweeping 15km downhill to Randuwa Bridge and the valley floor. The road follows the Seti River valley with a gently descending undulating gradient for 38km to the town of Dipayal. Cross the Seti Bridge, then turn immediately sharp right, and cross Dwari Khola Bridge for the last 12km climb up to the town of Silgadhi.

There are many food stalls and snack shops along the valley road. Recommended for hot food is Twins Café (the 45km point), 1.5km after Lowakhadi Bridge, on the left side of the road. The busy town of Dipayal

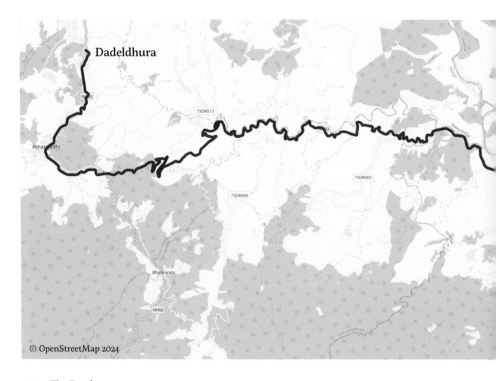

© OpenStreetMap 2024

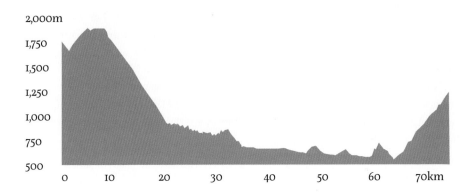

Elevation of Day 1.

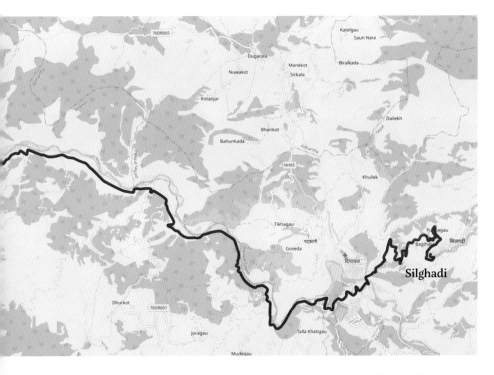

is also a good place to eat and stock up on supplies before the final 12km climb of the day to Silghadi.

Day 1 Journal Extract

Looking for an appropriate starting point for The Road was quite a challenge. It had to be in the far west, close to the Indian border. Dadeldhura was recommended for its location and amenities for stocking up for the start of the trip. Last night, we were told by a local that there was a festival in a nearby Hindu temple just a few kilometres out of town the very next day, so we decided to start early and take a look.

As we rolled our bikes down to Ugratara early in the morning, it became clear very quickly that it was going to be a special day. The road was filled with swarms of ladies in beautiful crimson saris gliding towards a mass of colour in the valley below. Young boys in pristine white shirts were jumping around with excitement as the crowds swarmed and thickened and we rolled further into a sea of colour, smoke and fragrant incense.

We dismounted the bikes and walked around the festival taking place in and around the temple. We seemed invisible to the pilgrims and worshippers – all entranced

Ugratara Temple, the Far West.

Tuk Tuk, Silghadi.

by this quite mystical religious occasion. The mass of people, the smoke, the smells, the stunning clothes and jewellery seemed so exotic and spiritual that it was hard not to get swept up with the spirit of the gathering. The vibrant colours of yellow, red and orange, so synonymous with Hindu culture, made the whole scene seem so bright and alive, together with exquisite flower arrangements and garlands conveying the love and dedication of the people to their religious beliefs. There were various sage-like figures dotted in and around the temple grounds who were giving blessings for a small donation. We were soon covered in red and yellow dust that fell from our foreheads onto our clothes as we wandered around. The atmosphere of life, colour, faith and positivity that we stumbled on by chance on this morning made us realise very quickly that the gates of Ugratara Temple were the perfect starting point for the long and difficult journey of The Road.

Recommended Places to Stay in Silgadhi

Hotel: Danfe Hotel
Room rate: 1200 NPR (twin share).
Meal prices: 300-400 NPR

Hotel: Khaptad Homestay
Room rate: 1000 NPR (twin share).
Meal prices: 300-400 NPR

The Far West.

Day 2: Silghadi – Sanfebagar

Distance: 63km

Cycling Time: 5.5hrs

Climbing: 1820m

Technical Level: 2/5

Endurance Level: 3/5

Route Summary

Made up of 90% paved route and 10% broken pavement and cobbles, A short and steep 1km climb through the charming, cobbled streets of the town followed by a steady 13km climb to Shanti Bazaar (1571m), a good place for tea and to pick up snacks. An 11km descent follows with great views of the rice terraced valley and farmers working their land with buffalo all the way to Sajhghat. It is recommended to stop here to refuel before the 16km (960m) climb to Chaukhutte (1882m), a good place for lunch at the various roadside stalls and food stands. A fast 25km paved descent follows to the valley floor and the town of Sanfebagar.

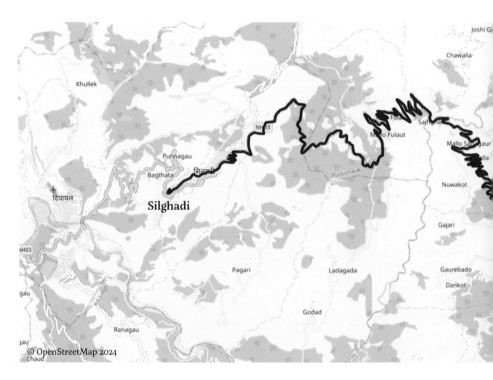

© OpenStreetMap 2024

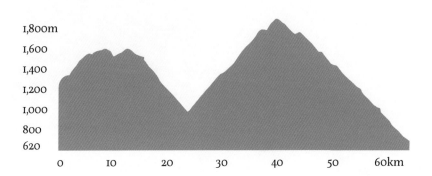

Elevation of Day 2.

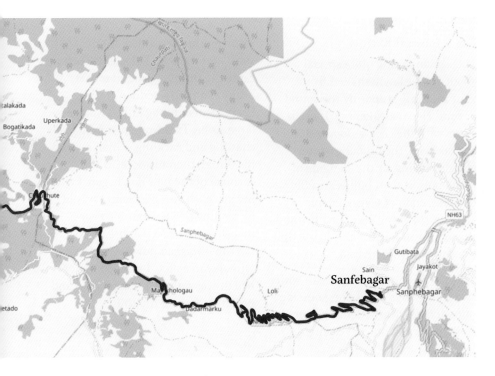

Viewpoint, near Silghadi.

Day 2 Journal Extract

There's something quite special about being slowly shaken from your morning stupor by the sound of rural Nepal awakening. It often starts with the cock-a-doodle-doo of a cockerel, the flippant banter of kids playing, or the clanging of metal pots. It then builds steadily to a crescendo of voices, people spitting, the firing up of engines and the tooting of horns – the signal that the day has truly arrived.

This particular morning began with two young boys squabbling outside our window, clearly fighting over something. One started crying.

Their mother screamed out in a shrill and the boys fell silent. Then came the thudding sound of wet, heavy slapping – sodden clothes being beaten dry against a wall or large stone. Two women started chatting and cackling, a man cleared his throat, then his nose, as the carnival of the new day began. I felt my stomach rumble. Soon I would be scoffing down scrambled eggs in a chapati – a Nepali breakfast burrito – washed down with fresh Himalayan coffee. I jumped out of bed (it was only our second day) and began to prepare my things.

Recommended Places to Stay in Sanfebagar

Hotel: New Dolphin Hotel
Room rate: 1800 NPR (twin share).
Meal prices: 400-500 NPR

Hotel: Hotel Saino and Lodge
Room rate: 450 NPR (per person).
Meal prices: 300-400 NPR

The Road to Sanfebagar.

The Road to Sanfebagar.

Day 3: Sanfebagar – Mangalsen

Distance: 31.5km

Cycling Time: 4.15hrs

Climbing: 1610m

Technical Level: 2/5

Endurance Level: 3/5

Route Summary

Mostly paved road with some broken sections and a small amount of unpaved sections.

There is a steady climb for 13km (570m ascent) out of Sanfebagar through dense forest, then an undulating high road for 3km (up to 1162m) before an 8km (596m) descent. You'll encounter many switchbacks and potholes and plenty of sand on the downhill, so ride with caution. At the river it's recommended to have a lunch break at one of the food stalls at Kailash Khola Bridge (the 21km point). Then there is a steep 11km climb (703m ascent), mostly paved, to the small mountain settlement of Mangalsen (1333m).

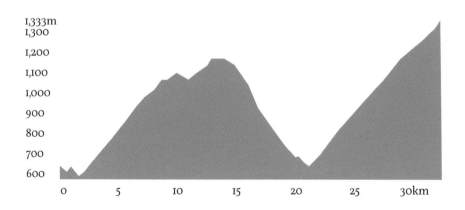

Elevation of Day 3.

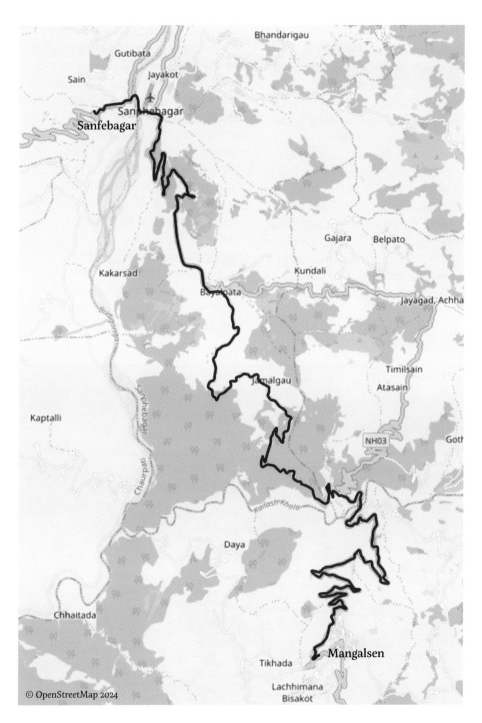

© OpenStreetMap 2024

Day 3 Journal Extract

Today it became very clear that the people of the far west of Nepal are not accustomed to seeing Western visitors. It's all in the look. In the more visited trekking areas of the country local people are immediately friendly – big smiles, pressed hands and namastes. But as we now ventured several days inland from the Indian border, deep into the far west, people's reactions began to change. They were more curious – often a frown instead of a smile. The children were sometimes suspicious and would run away.

On arrival in one tiny settlement, two young boys fled when they saw me, and one man stared me down for around ten seconds. He then burst out laughing. He called his friend over to come and look at this freak show that had just rolled into town. His friend took one look at me and laughed as well. I caught a glimpse of myself in a smudgy pane of glass, and they were right – I must have looked a sight in this remote, antiquated rural community – flash white helmet, glossy shades, middle-aged and sweating like a pig. I got off my bike for a breather and drank some water.

Before I had the chance to notice, in just a heartbeat, the two kids that had fled when they saw me moments earlier had now stolen my bike and were scarpering down the dusty track with it. The two men laughed again. One boy managed to mount the saddle and let out a cry of joy as he took off.

Recommended Places to Stay in Mangalsen

Hotel: Hotel Hillview
Room rate: 1500 NPR (double room).
Meal prices: 400-500 NPR

Hotel: Sunshine Hotel and Lodge
Room rate: 1000 NPR (twin share).
Meal prices: 300-400 NPR

Left and above: The Road to Mangelsen.

Taking a break, The Far West.

Day 4: Mangalsen – Sigaudi

Distance: 56.8km

Cycling Time: 6hrs

Climbing: 1740m

Technical Level: 3/5

Endurance Level: 5/5

Route Summary

A big day – be sure to carry plenty of snacks and water. A steep 12km (760m ascent) up to 2090m is followed by an undulating plateau for another 12km. This is followed by an exhilarating 22km descent to the Karnali River. It is recommended to have lunch at the food stalls before the Shai Khola Bridge (crossing the Kanali River). Following lunch there is a steady 10km climb (700m ascent) up to the hill station village of Sigaudi.

Typical rural home, the Far West.

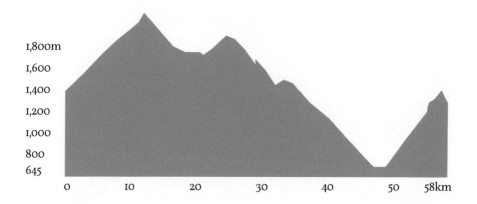

Elevation of Day 4.

Sigaudi.

Day 4 Journal Extract

There's a saying that goes, 'those with the least are often the most generous', and we certainly found this to be true today. It was a tough day, the miles accumulating in the legs, and the last climb of the day seemed to go on forever. Our guide, Om, had told us we would be camping in a Dalit community that night. Dalits are at the bottom of the pile of the south Asian Hindu Caste systems. They are the underclass, born into a perpetual cycle of poverty with no opportunity to improve their social status, to better themselves, no matter how good they are or how hard they work. Despite being outlawed in 1963, the Caste system is still deeply ingrained in Nepalese society. I guess that's why we were warned to be vigilant in Dalit areas, as they could, apparently, be volatile people. What we experienced was completely contrary. Since there were no hotels, guesthouses or even homestays in this poor community, we were guided by a local police officer and some curious locals to a small field where we were allowed to pitch our tents for the night. Before we had the chance to get cold (we were soaking wet from the last long climb) we were escorted to a small tin shack close by, where there was

a fire and a young lady called Laxmi cooking dal bhat. Two cold beers swiftly arrived for Mark and I, and some homemade popcorn appeared fresh from the fire. Mark and Laxmi had a chat using Google Translate. Lots of laughs and personal connection ensued, despite us being from completely different worlds to Laxmi, and her dal bhat was one of the tastiest we'd ever eaten. The next morning was a stunner – blazing sunshine and bright blue skies. We took a group photo with the whole community that would turn out to be one of the fondest memories of the entire trip.

Recommended Places to Stay in Sigaudi

At the time of publication there is no accommodation in Sigaudi, so camping is required. Check into the police checkpoint and they will guide you to a place where you can camp and will likely find a home that will cook for you. A very friendly village where western tourists are extremely rare, but very welcome.

Left and above: Sigaudi.

Sunset over the far-western hills.

Day 5: Sigaudi – Dailekh

Distance: 68km

Cycling Time: 6.5hrs

Climbing: 2320m

Technical Level: 4/5

Endurance Level: 5/5

Route Summary

A big day, with tough climbs and thrilling descents – four reasonable climbs with some steep sections and three downhill sections. The terrain is quite sandy, so ride cautiously.

Starting in Sigaudi, there is a small off-road section before joining the road eastbound.

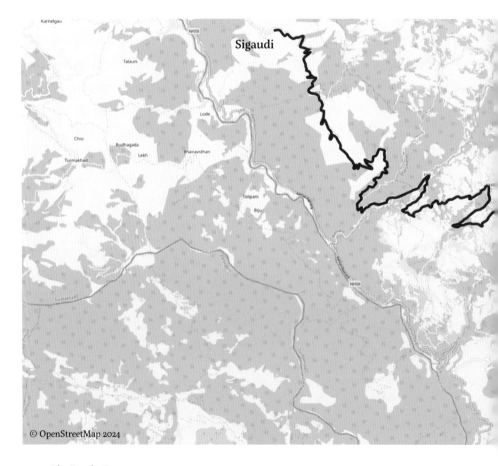

© OpenStreetMap 2024

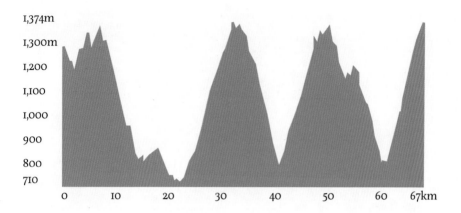

Elevation of Day 5.

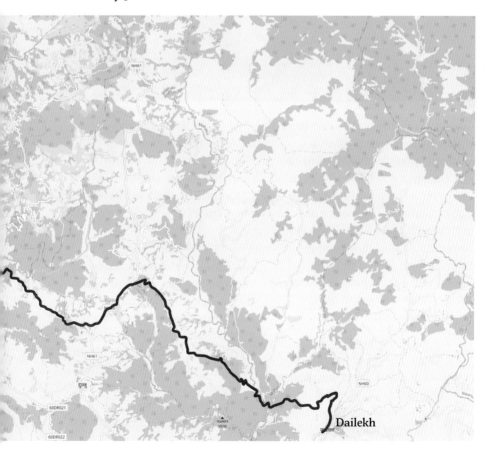

A steep 6km climb to the first peak of the day at Sattala (1358m) is followed by a 15km fast descent to Pull Bazaar, a good place for chai and to refuel before a 10km climb (660m ascent) to the second peak at 1373m. This is followed by a 8km descent to Padukastan Temple and an immediate 9km climb (580m ascent) to the third peak at Dullu village (1336m, the 50km point). Dullu is a good place to stop for lunch.

After lunch there is a small climb before a 12km fast, sweeping descent to Kholi Bazaar. It is possible to sleep here at Nandaram Homestay – basic but clean accommodation.

If you have the energy it is recommended to tackle the fourth climb of the day (7km, 585m ascent) up to the Bazaar town of Dailekh (1372m) where there are hotels with hot showers.

Day 5 Journal Extract

A hard day today, with lots of tea stops and people watching between the long climbs. Watching children playing in rural Nepal is a joyful sight. It seems so idyllic – the freedom, the mischief and fun in this warm, sun-dappled landscape. It appears like some kind of Tom Sawyer and Huck Finn adventure in every rural settlement. But one thing you come to realise is that there are very few young men of working age in western Nepal. It's striking. Most inhabitants are women, children and the elderly. I spoke to one old man at the lunch stop today and asked him where all the working men were. He said most men from these parts migrate to work in India or the Middle East into often tough jobs – labouring in searing heat, typically on huge construction sites with questionable safety standards. I remember reading, probably five years ago, that over 400 Nepali men had died on Qatar's World Cup football stadium building sites, a number that stuck with me, knowing how honest, kind and hardworking young Nepali men generally are. That number must be much higher today, the week the Qatar World Cup actually kicks off. As I pondered this grim statistic, a small group of boys were messing around in the field next door, laughing their heads off, as we sat watching, drinking our tea. Pure innocence, pure fun. It was impossible not to wonder what the future would hold for them.

Dailekh District.

Recommended Places to Stay in Dailekh

Hotel: Hotel Manosabar
Room rate: 2000 NPR (twin share).
Meal prices: 400-500 NPR

All photos: Dailekh District.

Day 6: Dailekh – Dashera

Distance: 61.5km

Cycling Time: 4.5hrs

Climbing: 2240m

Technical Level: 3/5

Endurance Level: 5/5

Route Summary

Quite a bumpy 10km descent (stony jeep track) from Dailekh to Lohore Lamtada Bazaar is followed by a picturesque and undulating 14km paved ascent to the settlement of Bestada Bazaar. It is recommended to have lunch here at the Thapa Hotel, before a challenging but paved 20km climb up to 2374m, the highest point of the day. Here the land becomes more sparse and exposed at the higher altitudes. A warm layer may be needed for the 16km descent (with one steep 2.5km, 200m climb) to the small settlement of Dashera (1760m).

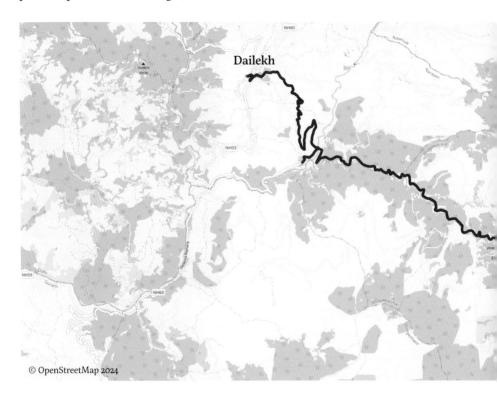

© OpenStreetMap 2024

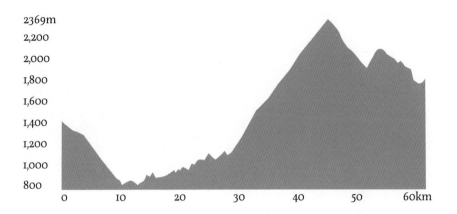

Elevation of Day 6.

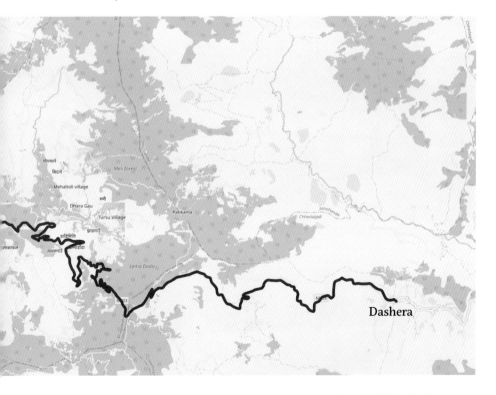

The Raute people.

The open road.

Day 6 Journal Extract

During breakfast, Om was busy on the phone, talking more colourfully than usual. He had caught wind of a group of Raute people living nearby temporarily. The Raute are the last nomadic people of Nepal and are extremely elusive, as they move location every four to five months and inhabit lands in the deeper areas of rural west Nepal. The latest census identified only 52 families (about 180 individuals) of these nomadic people left in Nepal. Om informed us that the Raute eat macaque monkey and langur as their staple, and in the subsequent sentence told us that we were going to visit them after breakfast. I can't say I wasn't a little nervous; they sounded, quite literally, wild. But we trusted Om, and off we went.

As we peddled towards the settlement deep in the hills, my mouth went dry and my heart thumped with an uncomfortable edge. We were met at the entrance to the camp (the Raute live under tarpaulin canopies propped up by wooden poles) by a smiling old man with a face that told a thousand stories. He welcomed us warmly and, after exchanging pleasantries with Om, allowed us to enter the community. Young children walked curiously down the dusty hills to see what the commotion was all about. They stopped a safe distance away and just stared at us. I motioned to one young girl of around ten years old to ask if it was OK for me to take her photo. Her hair was matted with unkempt dreadlocks and her ocean-blue cardigan and exquisite jewellery made her glow with a strange beauty. She kind of nodded, I think, but kept frowning at me, trying to figure me out. I raised my camera, and her expression didn't change. I took one photo, but it felt uncomfortable. I put the camera away.

This evening, flicking through the photos from the day, I kept going back to that image.

Recommended Place to Stay in Dashera

Hotel: Homestay (opposite Health Post)
Room rate: 500 NPR (twin share).
Meal prices: 400-500 NPR

Below: Raute girl.

En route to the Raute community.

The Raute people.

The Raute people.

Ghanta – Hindu ritual and prayer bells.

West Central Nepal.

Young Hindu scholars.

Day 7: Dashera – Jajarkot

Distance: 76km

Cycling Time: 7hrs

Climbing: 1655m

Technical Level: 4/5

Endurance Level: 5/5

Route Summary

An undulating 4km climb before a sweeping and fast 10km descent with stunning views of wide-open valleys. Be wary of sand and gravel. A picturesque and quite technical 28km of undulating jeep track along the Bheri River follows, until you join the quiet single-lane highway at Cheda Bazaar, a good stop to refuel. From there, there is an undulating 22km paved road to Phera Kola, a good place for lunch before the steady 10km climb (600m ascent) to the Bazaar hill station town of Jajarkot.

The Bheri River.

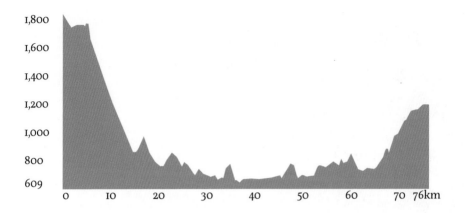

Elevation of Day 7.

© OpenStreetMap 2024

Sunset, West Central Nepal.

Day 7 Journal Extract

In the hotel this evening we met a local social worker who was telling us about the practice of Chhaupadi in this region. This practice is based on a centuries-old belief that women and girls are unclean and untouchable during menstruation. They are not allowed to do a range of activities, and in some cases are banished to 'period huts' for the duration. The practice is deeply embedded in western Nepal, especially in the more remote hills to the north of Jajarkot, just a stone's throw from where we were riding today. Many young women have died over the years in these huts, mostly from snake bites, smoke inhalation in windowless huts or fire. Chhaupadi was outlawed in 2005, punishable by up to three months in prison and a 3,000 Nepali rupee (£20) fine, but is still known to take place in some of the more remote regions of western Nepal. In 2019, the practice caused national outrage when a young woman of 21, along with her two young sons, died from suffocation after spending three nights in a period hut. Her death was the fifth reported case that year. These tragic deaths became national news, which led to high-profile programmes and campaigns to end the practice. Thousands of period huts were destroyed, but when Covid arrived the momentum to banish the practice completely was reportedly lost. As people stopped talking about it, the huts were steadily reinstated, and last year, in 2023, another death was reported. The social worker said it's very hard to completely abolish due to the remoteness of many settlements, but they are trying to track down and educate communities still involved in the practice, and prosecute when necessary.

Recommended Place to Stay in Jajarkot

Hotel: Hotel Himalayan
Room rate: 1500 NPR (twin share).
Meal prices: 500-600 NPR

Jajarkot District.

All photos: Jajarkot District.

Day 8: Jajarkot – Musikot

Distance: 43km

Cycling Time: 4.5hrs

Climbing: 1654m

Technical Level: 2/5

Endurance Level: 3/5

Route Summary

Head east from the hotel through the town, past Jajarkot district hospital and Kalegaun. Keep descending and cross the visible long suspension bridge over the Bheri River (the 7km point). Hike your bike up the river bank and turn LEFT at the road.

Then there is a long, undulating, fast and fun paved section along the river (on your left side), passing Chaina Bazaar, Sahare, Simli (a good stop for drinks and snacks) to Chutara (at 32km). This is a good place to stop for lunch (recommended: the Durbar restaurant left side of road) before a steep 10km climb (690m ascent) to the small hill station of Musikot.

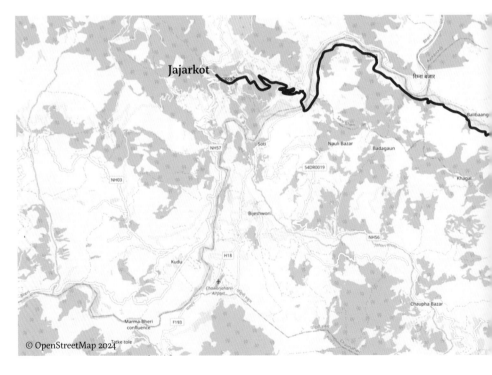

© OpenStreetMap 2024

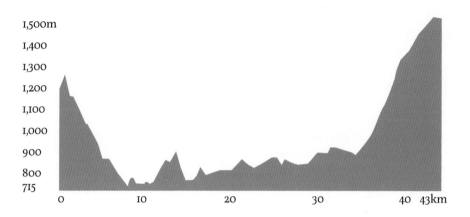

Elevation of Day 8.

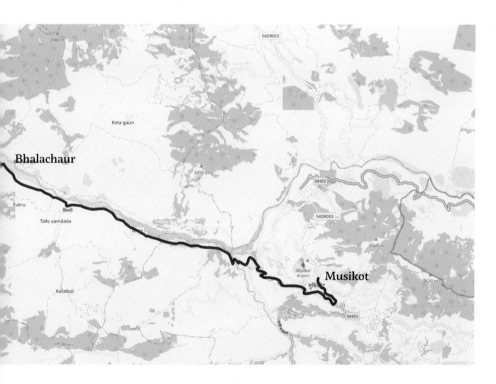

Day 8 Journal Extract

A relatively short day today, so we arrived early and decided to head out into town for beers and momos. Musikot is a moody little hill town with high, ramshackle buildings where very little natural light reaches the streets. Kids scarpered around like Dickensian street urchins and groups of men drank cheap spirits behind bilious curtains in dimly lit bars, while the women kept the town together, closing things up for the day. We met a guy in a bar who spoke good English and told us a remarkable tale. Over the past three years, he'd paid over 40,000 US dollars to Nepali 'relocation agents' to try to get (smuggle) him into the USA. On his journey to the Promised Land, he'd been literally sent off unwittingly on a baffling global odyssey of flights that took him to the Middle East, Madrid, Costa Rica, Honduras, Paris, Nigeria, Delhi, back to Paris, Senegal, Bombay and back to Kathmandu...

This was just his first attempt, which cost him 20,000 dollars. The second attempt was equally mind-bending, visiting some of those destinations again, as well as others, on another world tour.

Musikot.

Musikot.

He never even got close to a US border, and now here he was sat, back home in rural west Nepal, having spent his family's wealth (selling off land and property) on a con that apparently destroys many Nepali lives and dreams. These unofficial relocation agents obviously work in a murky world, so there is no regulation or accountability. From what we heard from other drinkers in the bar, some are genuine smugglers with some record of success, while others are not. This poor fellow sitting in front of us tonight fell foul to the latter, being sent on a wild goose chase of cheap, aimless flights to help justify and hide the con he was being subjected to. The odd thing was, this man thought his agent did the best he could to get him to the US, still not believing the agent would have ripped him off. This unconditional trust that desperate people put in these con artists selling the imaginary dream is abused beyond comprehension. As organised crimes go, this one is pretty damn low.

Recommended Places to Stay in Musikot

Hotel: Asian Hotel
Room rate: 1500 NPR (twin share).
Meal prices: 400-500 NPR

The smoky Mid Hills.

Day 9: Musikot – Rukumkot

Distance: 37.2km

Cycling Time: 3.5hrs

Climbing: 1476m

Technical Level: 2/5

Endurance Level: 2/5

Route Summary

A shorter day, but don't be fooled by the short distance. After a 2km descent there is a long and relentless climb (920m ascent), all paved, for 15km up to Rindat (2390m). This is a very quiet section of high road. It can be cold up top, so have a wind jacket for the fun descent, which is mostly paved for approximately 8km before you cross the valley and follow an undulating descent for 5km before the final descent to the settlement of Rukumkot.

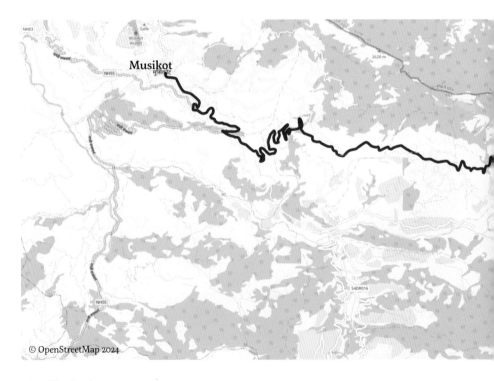

© OpenStreetMap 2024

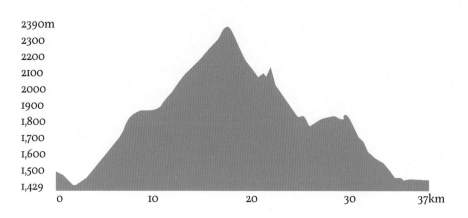

Elevation of Day 9.

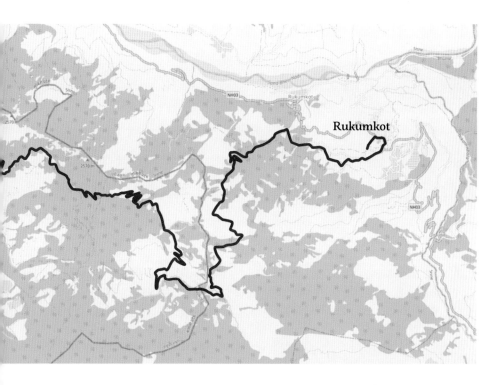

Rukumkot

Rukum District.

Rukum District.

Day 9 Journal Extract

Another relatively short day, with one monster climb. Felt the legs today, so it was a joy to roll down into a warm, green valley under the amber glow of the afternoon sun to the newly built Lake City Hotel. The hotel was a huge, modern, sky-blue cube that looked like it had recently landed on the ancient flood plain from another planet.

Its juxtaposition against a farmer working his ox in the neighbouring field was an odd one, but we didn't ponder for long as we were escorted to our room on the second floor of the hotel. The room was also huge: two double beds, bedside tables, a desk, a balcony shimmering in the afternoon heat, a real sit-down toilet and a warm shower, plus Wi-Fi! It was nothing too fancy by Western standards, basic and functional, probably two or three-star, but to us it felt like five-star luxury. It's funny how quickly relativity sets in and rewires our brains to cope with situations, to regulate our expectations to deal with relative hardships.

Over the past week we had become accustomed to funky stand-up loos in tiny, neck-bending shacks, no electricity in our rooms, no heating, washboard beds and, God forbid, no Wi-Fi. But we coped and just got on with it, and memories of these relative hardships will no doubt remain fond to us for the fact that they were different and shook us out of our spoilt, western-comfort malaise for short moments.

Both Mark and I showered and washed some clothes and hung them to dry on the hot stone balcony, knowing we would be cycling tomorrow in clean kit for the first time in days – a small victory we cherished. We sat back and sank a cold beer as the setting sun dried our hair and warmed our faces.

Recommended Place to Stay in Rukumkot

Hotel: Lake City Hotel
Room rate: 1500 NPR (twin share).
Meal prices: 500-600 NPR

Day 10: Rukumkot – Burtibang

Distance: 85km

Cycling Time: 6hrs

Climbing: 1925m

Technical Level: 2/5

Endurance Level: 5/5

Route Summary

A long day – leave early (no later than 7.30am). Consisting of 90% paved road, this section begins with a short climb out of the Rukumkot is followed by a 4km descent, then a picturesque undulating ascent along the valley floor, twisting through valley after valley.

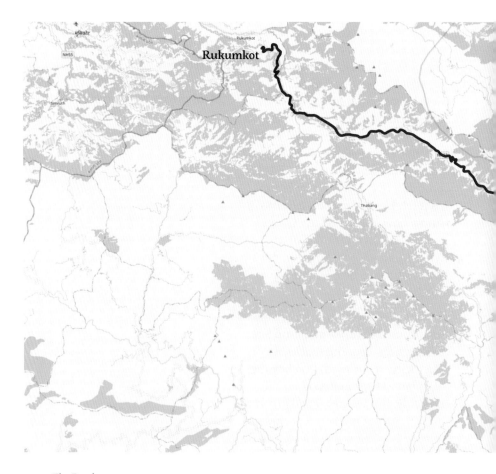

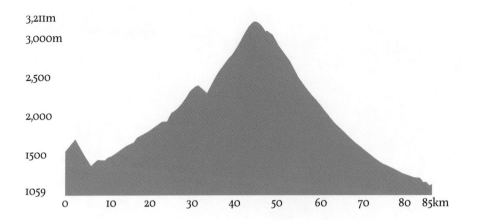

Elevation of Day 10.

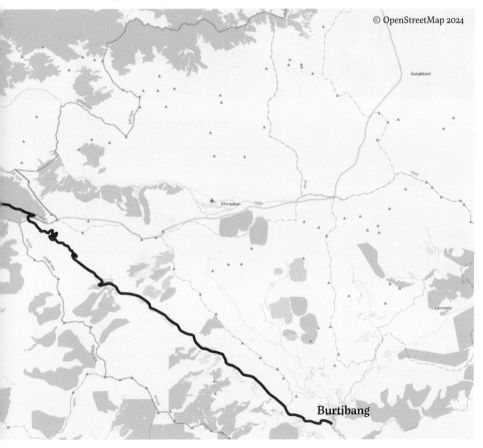

Above: Momo lady and steamed momos, near Burtibang.

Khabang Bazaar, at 18km, is a good place to stop for tea and snacks. Load up on calories and fluids here before you start to climb. The first peak is at 31km (2370m), followed by a short descent before a 13km climb to Patihalne Pass (3209m). It will likely be cold on top and breezy, so layer up for the thrilling descent, a fast 40km gauntlet all the way to the valley floor settlement of Burtibang. The recommended hotel, Famous Hotel, is not situated in the town but just right off the final bridge (Bhuji Khola) before the climb into Burtibang.

Day 10 Journal Extract

A screamer of a day, pushed to the limits both physically and mentally, with some big climbs taking us over 3000m into a sparser landscape and a thinner air that really lets you know you are in the Himalayas. We arrived at the day's summit – Patihalne Pass (3209m) – later than expected, around 3pm. It was cold, and we were soaked with sweat from the relentless climbing in the hot sun. Contours of body salt swirled around my base layer like snail-trails, so I whipped off my top and replaced it with a warm, dry fleece for the 40km descent to Burtibang. It was a cosmic descent

– sweeping, fast Nepali life flashing by like old sepia film slides. As we dropped, the air warmed, and we looked for every opportunity to pop some air on the roadside like excited, adolescent BMX bandits. We regrouped near the bottom, 4km from our destination, and spotted a small snack shop. We were famished and in need of reward. We dropped our bikes and went inside the walled yard, where the hatch of goodies was on display. On the left as we entered there was a man sitting on a plastic chair under a tree eating what looked like some of the best steamed momos I'd ever seen. Behind him was a big window with chicken wire for its pane. We peered through it, and inside there was a middle-aged Tibetan-looking lady with two massive metal steamers knocking out plates of what looked like world-class momos in this unremarkable kitchen on the side of a single-track road, 4km from the nearest town. We were so hungry that we ordered a plate each and crunched some cheesy puffs from the snack shop for entrée. We were there for about an hour and throughout this time many local people wandered in for a plate of these delicious momos and sat in the plastic chairs under the overhanging tree to enjoy them for a quiet moment before going back to their daily business.

On the road to Burtibang.

Tonight, I couldn't help but wonder how many of these places exist throughout the Himalayan foothills, serving up food from the most basic kitchens that could hold their own in the best restaurants in Europe. We must have bombed past scores of them since our journey began, but I guess that's the joy of travel and discovery – a series of random encounters and experiences that provide each of us with our own unique stories to tell.

Recommended Place to Stay in Burtibang

Hotel: Famous Hotel
Room rate: 2000 NPR (twin share).
Meal prices: 500-600 NPR

Left and above: The road to Burtibang.

Day 11: Burtibang – Galkot

Distance: 42.1km

Cycling Time: 3hrs

Climbing: 770m

Technical Level: 2/5

Endurance Level: 2/5

Route Summary

One of the less intense days, but it can be very hot. This low-altitude ride (much of it below 1000m) gives way to subtropical flora and the sound of cicadas as you weave along the valley floors.

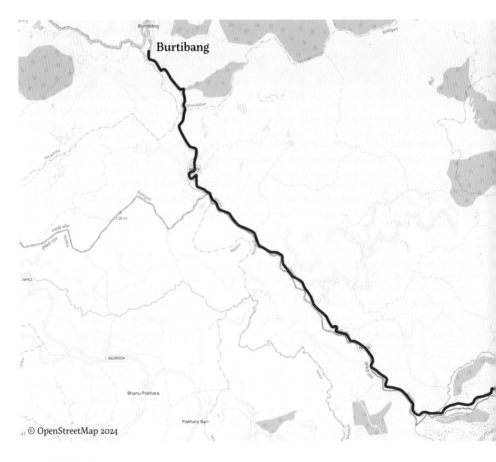

Burtibang

© OpenStreetMap 2024

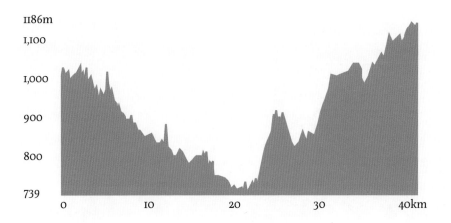

Elevation of Day 11.

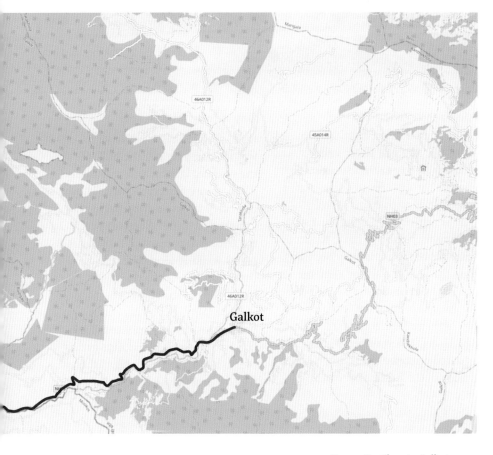

Galkot

Collecting grass, near Galkot.

A sweeping 22km (500m) undulating descent from Burtibang along the Badigad River valley before a steady 24km ascent begins, passing through beautiful, peaceful countryside with many small bazaar settlements along the route (Bhimgithe, Khala, Khara, Nwara), with lots of food and drink options. Pass through the sleepy settlements of Timurbot and Bans Khola before the final short descent into the colourful and quiet town of Galkot. The Hotel & Restaurant Monsoon is situated opposite the Gaudi Khola Bridge in the middle of town.

Day 11 Journal Extract

It's a common sight in Nepal to see women carrying out the bulk of the manual labour, and very often it's the more elderly women. They can carry loads on their backs that almost defy belief. Every day on the trip we have passed numerous ladies walking along the side of the roads, backs hunched with huge loads of dried grass on them, strapped on tight with a cotton band across their foreheads. From behind they look like walking trees in full bloom, their wiry, weathered legs the scarpering trunks.

The grass is to feed the goats and the buffaloes – a tough daily task in the countryside. The nature of the landscape makes it hard for the clumsy buffalo to go to the field to graze. Buffalo are a prized possession in a Nepali family and in some castes a young girl is bonded with a young buffalo and will look after that animal for life. This is due to the finicky nature of the animals, so looking after them is a well-learned skill!

Today we timed a chai stop by chance at the same time as a group of four ladies carrying grass loads. They filled the quiet road as they approached the tea shop, side by side, and all four broke out with huge smiles when we greeted them. Om and Manish engaged in some lively banter, and before we knew it Manish jumped up and looped the cotton strap of one of the loads around his forehead and attempted to lift it up onto his back. After a bit of a wobble with his body fully jack-knifed forward, he managed it, but you could tell by the look on his face it was a struggle. The women all cackled as he stumbled with his load down the road like a drunk. Then Mark fancied his chances and decided to give it a go as well. He managed, with a bit of support from

Waterfall, Galkot Municipality.

one of the ladies, to hoist a load onto his back. It was a fun moment, everyone in and around the tea shop was in stitches, but when the boys returned the two loads to the ladies, the relief on their red faces was clear and the nods of respect they gave the ladies as they returned to their bikes were palpable.

Recommended Place to Stay in Galkot

Hotel: Monsoon Hotel
Room rate: 2000 NPR (twin share).
Meal prices: 500-600 NPR

Above and right: The Annapurna range.

Day 12: Galkot – Kushma

Distance: 68km

Cycling Time: 4.5hrs

Climbing: 780m

Technical Level: 2/5

Endurance Level: 3/5

Route Summary

A long, steady climb of 18km up to the Galkot lookout tower pass (2150m) will reward you with spectacular views of Dhaulagiri and the Annapurna Himalaya range.

Following this is a long, sweeping, undulating descent for over 40km with snow-capped Himalayan views all the way down. At the 47km point in Baglung, you can visit the Gandaki Golden Footbridge over the Kaligandaki River, the longest suspension bridge in Nepal.

This area sees relatively heavy traffic as you head towards Pokhara, and lots of dust, so be cautious. Kushma is a small suburban town of Pokhara with many options for food and drink.

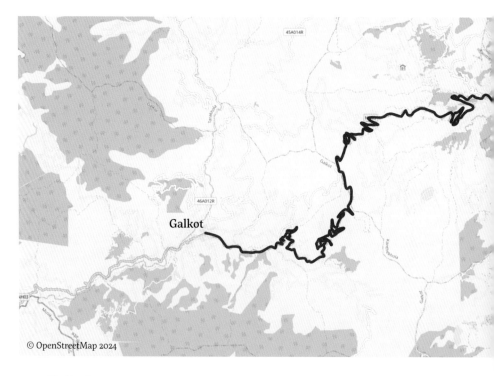

© OpenStreetMap 2024

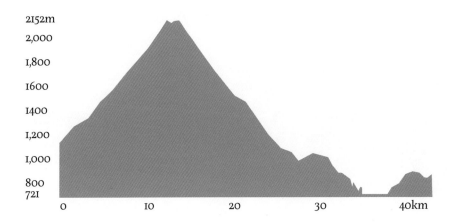

Elevation of Day 12.

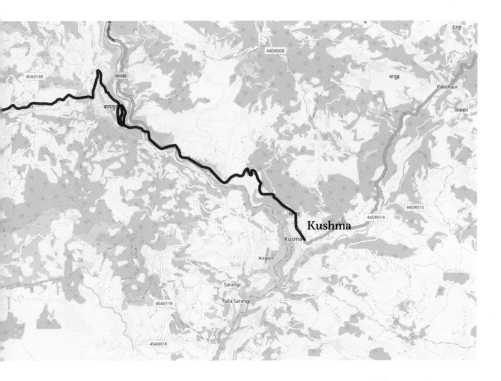

Dhaulagiri, the eighth highest mountain in the world.

Day 12 Journal Extract

A rude awakening – a soul asphyxiating climb of 18km with tired legs, aching back and sores. Sun cream oozed from my sweaty brow into my eyes compounding my general pain and misery. But we knew that this big climb was our last for this first section of The Road. I was in the granny ring for most of it, traversing back and forth across the road at a snail's pace just to ensure I would make it. I could have probably walked the bike at a faster pace. After what seemed like an eternity, we reached the top, the Kalkot lookout tower, which seemed like an unremarkable pass in the mountains until we looked up. There it was, on this perfect bright blue day – the Annapurna Himalayan range in all its majesty, with Dhaulagiri, the eighth highest mountain on the planet, looming over us from what seemed only a stone's throw away. It was a stop-the-traffic moment. We dismounted our bikes on the side of the road, shattered, and stood for minutes, quietly taking it all in. Living close to the Alps, I'm used to seeing snow-capped peaks, but the scale of the Himalayas by comparison is striking. It really is like a land of giants. It was an emotional moment, not just seeing the high Himalayas for the first time on the trip, but because we knew the hard work was done, 12 days of solid riding and endless climbing, but now we just had the long run down to our destination of Pokhara ahead of us. Mark and I both had mixed feelings, happy to have made it but sad that this first section of The Road was drawing to its end.

Recommended Place to Stay in Kushma

Hotel: Hotel Mountain View Inn
Contact: hotel.kushma@gmail.com
Room rate: 2000 NPR (twin share).
Meal prices: 500-600 NPR

Gandaki Golden Footbridge, Nepal's longest suspension bridge.

Day 13: Kushma – Pokhara

Distance: 59km

Cycling Time: 2.5hrs

Climbing: 918m

Technical Level: 1/5

Endurance Level: 2/5

Route Summary

Undulating paved road for 12km before a long 16km (800m ascent) to Paudurkot, then a busy and congested 31km road into the beautiful lakeside town of Pokhara.

Day 13 Journal Extract

We were well and truly back into civilisation today since crossing the Galkot pass and dropping down into the Pokhara Valley. Cars swarmed the roads – heat, dust, the symphony of horns. We were bottom of the food chain on our bikes, so we rode with caution, dodging potholes, TATA trucks and women carrying huge stacks of grass on their heads. I cast my mind back over the past 12 days, trying to remember each one individually, but it was a struggle.

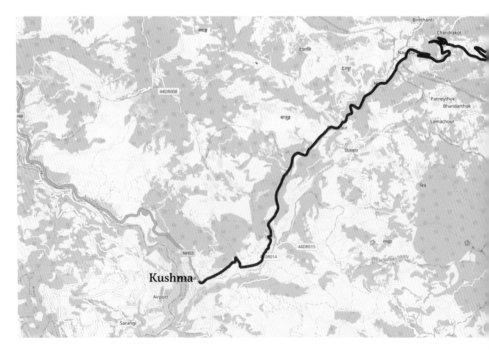

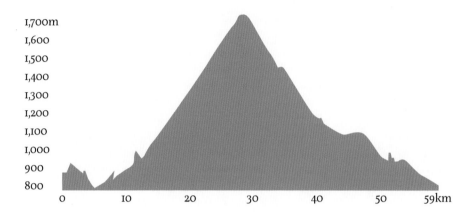

Elevation of Day 13.

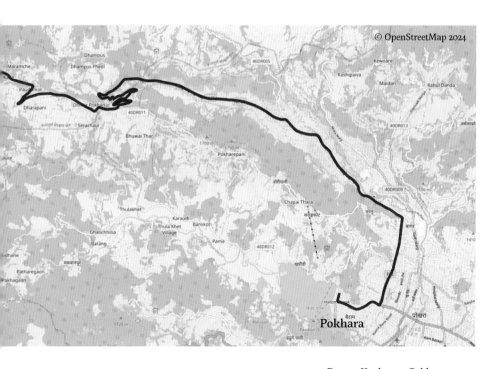

Phewa Tal, or Fewa Lake,
a mountain lake in Pokhara.

If I hadn't taken notes to remind me, it would likely have all gelled into one long, blurry day. Having spent so long in my thoughts cycling alone for much of the past days, I felt quite alien suddenly surrounded by so much life; an assault on the senses at every turn – people, machines, colours, sights, smells, heat... all encompassing. I felt in the thick of it, yet completely estranged from all the goings on, like a ghost gliding through the mayhem of urban Nepal.

We reached the enchanting lakeside city of Pokhara mid-afternoon, embraced with joy and relief and then took our time to let the moment sink in.

Recommended Place to Stay in Pokhara

There are many good options for hotels in Pokhara on booking.com.

Hotel: Hotel City Inn
Room rate: 3500 NPR (twin share).
Meal prices: 500-600 NPR

THE ROAD SECTION 2
Pokhara – Bhojpur
Days 14-29

Days 14-29
Pokhara – Phidim Bazaar

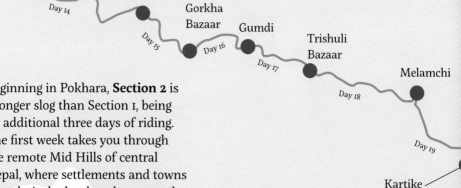

Pokhara

Paudi Bazaar

Day 14

Gorkha
Bazaar

Day 15

Gumdi

Day 16

Trishuli
Bazaar

Day 17

Melamchi

Day 18

Day 19

Kartike
Deurali

Da

Beginning in Pokhara, **Section 2** is a longer slog than Section 1, being an additional three days of riding. The first week takes you through the remote Mid Hills of central Nepal, where settlements and towns are relatively developed compared to the far west. But don't be fooled, the central Mid Hills remain remote and challenging, so prepare yourself every morning for a tough day ahead. The central regions are steeped in history, most notably the Gorkha region. Gorkha is the birthplace of Prithvi Narayan Shah, the Gorkha king that unified the territories of Nepal in the mid- to late eighteenth century, creating what is now considered modern Nepal. He became the first monarch of the Kingdom. His soldiers were also the warriors that developed over centuries to become the modern-day Gurkha soldiers, widely considered to be some of the most

fierce and feared army regiments on the planet. As you head out to the far east, you enter the lands of the Rai and Limbu people, very proud peoples with a rich cultural heritage. Clothing and architecture are particularly vibrant, and a strong sense of civic pride can be sensed as you travel through the settlements. And don't miss East Nepal's greatest export – the mighty Tongba! A warm alcoholic beverage made from fermented millet that will warm the cockles of your heart after a long day on the bike.

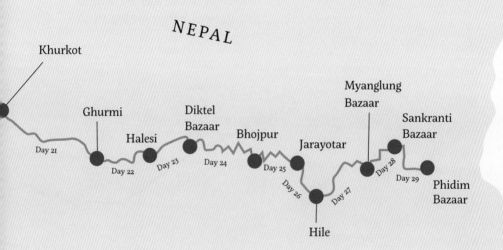

NEPAL

Khurkot

Ghurmi

Halesi

Diktel
Bazaar

Bhojpur

Jarayotar

Myanglung
Bazaar

Sankranti
Bazaar

Phidim
Bazaar

Hile

Day 21

Day 22

Day 23

Day 24

Day 25

Day 26

Day 27

Day 28

Day 29

NEPAL

The complete GPX files for the entire route are available for free to all those who buy the book. Recommended for use with Strava, Garmin or similar reputable digital mapping applications.

Day 14: Pokhara – Paudi Bazaar

Distance: 75km

Cycling Time: 6hrs

Climbing: 1604m

Technical Level: 4/5

Endurance Level: 3/5

Route Summary

Expect some traffic for the first 10km before turning off and steadily climbing into the mountains through the lush foothills and busy villages up beside Begnas Lake.

A flowing, undulating paved road for 30km follows, hot and subtropical with lots of banana plantations, before hitting an

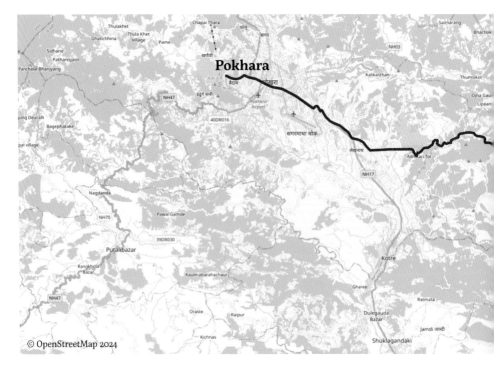

© OpenStreetMap 2024

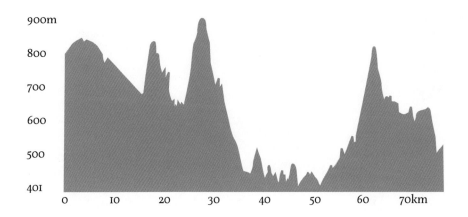

Elevation of Day 14.

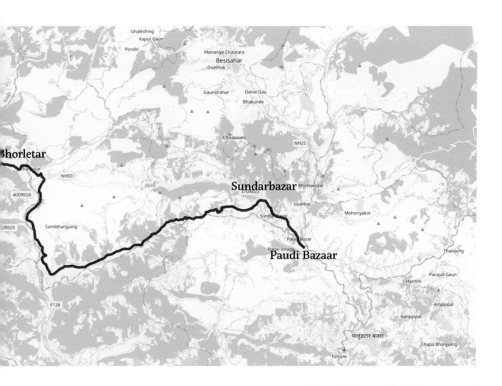

Climbing into the hills outside Pokhara.

unpaved section (several kms are technical) which climbs for 15km up to the settlement of Paudi Bazaar. A good stop for lunch is Bhorletar Lamjung (38km from the start).

When you arrive at the town, bear right down the hill on the road to Dumre, the hotel is 700m on the next hill, on the left side of the road.

Day 14 Journal Extract

Last night before our departure, Pokhara twinkled with lights. It's Tihar festival (in India it's known as Diwali) the festival of lights, which celebrates the triumph of light over darkness, good over evil and the human ability to overcome.

The festival is associated with Lakshmi, the Hindu goddess of wealth, prosperity and good fortune. It is customarily celebrated for five days. The streets bustled with excited families all beautifully dressed – ladies in crimson saris and children smart and colourful. On the streets outside the town's shopfronts, shop owners were hand painting intricate 'rangoli' designs – a form of symmetric Hindu folk art that made the streets truly come alive with colour. Many groups of children sang the traditional folk song called Deusi Bhailo (the Deusi is customarily performed by men and the Bhailo by women) while

Banana plantations in the subtropical lowlands.

Winding up towards Begnas Lake.

dancing on the dimly lit pavements and inside shops, to receive blessings and to collect money, as is customary during Tihar.

A real sense of positivity was in the air as we went to bed, knowing we had an early start the next morning. We woke excited, energised by the positive vibes from the festivities and set off, jostling our way through the early morning traffic of Pokhara on our bikes, the only urban riding stretch along the entire length of The Road. Cars and trucks snaked and swerved, horns blared, thick clouds of matt black exhaust fumes blasted out of the undercarriage of brightly coloured trucks, re-awakening all of our senses as we pulled steadily away from the crowded, polluted roads and up and up into the freshening air of the foothills, with shimmering Himalayan peaks soaring high into the sky in the distance.

Recommended Place to Stay in Paudi Bazaar

Hotel: Greenfields Cottage Guesthouse +977 985 604 0885
Room rate: 2000 NPR (twin share).
Meal prices: 350-450 NPR

Above: Noodle soup, scrambled eggs and momos – lunch of champions.

Right: Picking radishes.

Day 15: Paudi Bazaar – Gorkha Bazaar

Distance: 47km

Cycling Time: 4hrs

Climbing: 1295m

Technical Level: 2/5

Endurance Level: 3/5

Route Summary

A pleasant day of riding. Undulating paved road most of the way with several unpaved sections which are not too challenging and climbs that are not too long. A good lunch stop is Chepetar Gorkha (31km from the start), next to the river.

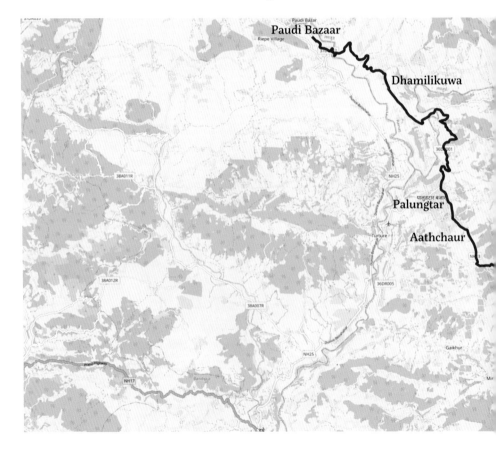

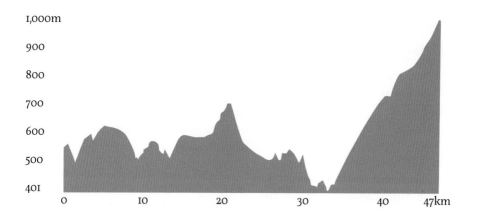

Elevation of Day 15.

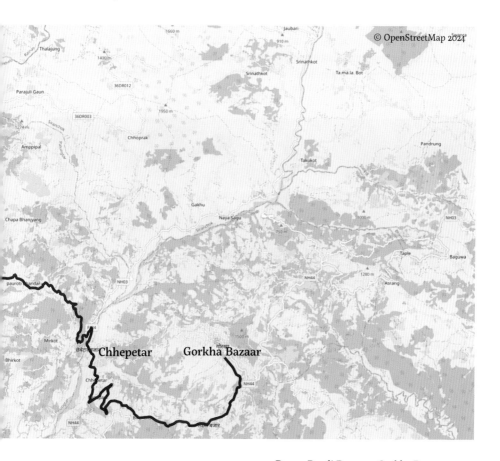

The last 12km climb up to Gorkha is the toughest section of the day.

Day 15 Journal Extract

Today was 'Bhai Tika' – the fifth and final day of the Tihar festival – celebrated in Nepal as 'siblings festival' day. Traditionally, it's the day when brothers travel back to see their sisters in their home village or region, and the sisters place a multi-coloured 'tika' on their foreheads as a sign of gratitude for protecting them, and as a wish for their brothers to become strong and powerful. There were very few shops open and there was nobody working on the land, a rare sight in rural Nepal. A true public holiday feel was in the air as we rode into the quiet hills. Communities gathered together, fathers and children played in the streets, also an uncommon sight in the heat of the day, and there was a real sense of peace in the usually bustling town of Gorkha when we arrived late in the afternoon.

Soon after arrival, while drinking our customary post-ride Gorkha beer, we were notified of the significance of the town in Nepal's history. I had a little Google to find out more.

Gorkha is the birthplace of Prithvi Narayan Shah, the Gorkha king that unified the territories of Nepal in

Fruit and veg, Central Nepal.

Rice harvesting with machines, Central Nepal.

the mid- to late eighteenth century, creating what is now considered modern Nepal. He became the first monarch of the kingdom.

Known as the 'land of the brave warrior', Gorkha is also the original home region of the world-famous Gurkha soldiers. The story of the Gurkhas, and how they came to have their own regiment in the British army, is quite a fascinating one. Gurkha warriors first encountered the invading Brits in the Gurkha War of 1814-1816, which ended not just in stalemate but with a strong sense of mutual respect and admiration between the two sides. The Peace Treaty that ended

Quality control.

Roadside chai stop, Gorkha District.

the war enabled Gurkhas to serve in the East India Company's army, which in turn became part of the British Army. Since then, more than 200,000 Gurkhas fought in the two World Wars and in the past 50 years, many have fought in battles across the globe, earning a strong reputation as being an elite force of fierce and loyal soldiers.

The number of serving Gurkhas now stands at around 2,800, with a place in the regiment still held as one of the most prestigious aspirations and achievements for young Nepali men.

Since 2015, women have also been permitted to join the Gurkhas, going through the same rigorous recruitment process as the men. The numbers are still small by comparison (at the time of writing, women make up around 3% of the regiment), but the British Army has implemented policies and training to support and promote equality and inclusion.

Recommended Place to Stay in Gorkha Bazaar

Hotel: Gorkha Palace +977 064421442
Room rate: 2500 NPR (twin share).
Meal prices: 300-400 NPR

Day 16: Gorkha Bazaar – Gumdi

Distance: 56km

Cycling Time: 4.5hrs

Climbing: 1073m

Technical Level: 3/5

Endurance Level: 3/5

Route Summary

After a short, steep, paved start, the road levels out to an undulating paved road for approximately 28km with great views of the white Himalayan peaks in the distance. Then follows a big, sweeping 10km descent to the town of Aarughat. This is a good lunch stop with several options. After lunch begins a largely unpaved stretch, mostly flat and bumpy with some paved sections, then one tough climb and a singletrack section through some fields and banana plantations,

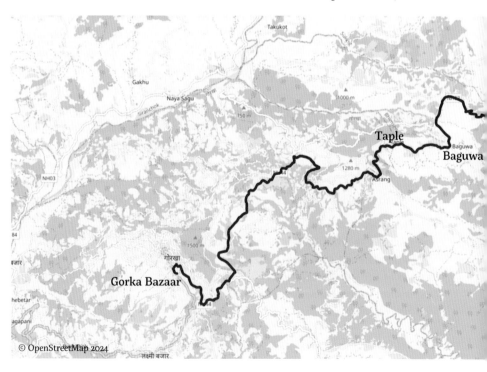

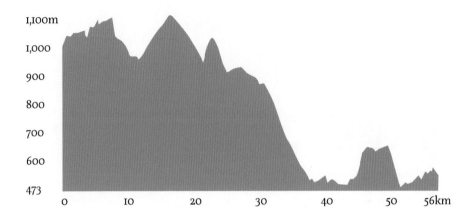

Elevation of Day 16.

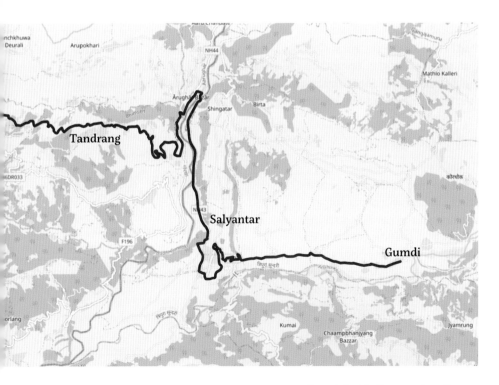

Sunset over the Mid Hills.

back onto road and track to the end of the ride at the rural Gumdi guesthouse (the 56km point) on the right-hand side of the stony track (the sign is quite hidden, be careful not to miss it!).

Day 16 Journal Extract

Today's ride took us close to the epicentre of the tragic 2015 earthquake. I will never forget turning on the news and seeing the scale of that disaster unfold. Less than two years prior to the earthquake, I had taken part in the Yak Attack mountain bike race that went through the Gorkha region (and then up and around the Annapurna Circuit) and had made friends with several of the

Nepali riders. I quickly learned that several of the riders' families and friends had been badly affected by the earthquake, which I remember thinking at the time must have been such a desperate situation due to the poor levels of communication in those remote mountains.

Last week, before we headed out of Kathmandu, we had a chance meeting with a retired Irish chap in a bike shop who told us he had been living in Nepal for several years, mostly working on earthquake preparedness and awareness. We told him where we were going, and he gave us a few tips on how to react in the extremely unlikely event we were to experience an earthquake

– if outside, run to a clearing away from buildings; be mindful of falling objects; if firmly inside a building, do not try to run out of it, but move away from the ground floor onto the first floor (poorly constructed buildings often collapse onto their ground floors); if in a high rise building, try to quickly descend to at least the third floor (the maximum length for universal ladders); spread onto your hands and knees and take shelter under a strong framed structure, like a table, if possible. All good tips, but, thankfully, none we had to during this trip (or on five or six previous rides through the region).

While it's prudent to be aware of and prepared for natural disasters, the infrequency and remote likelihood of ever experiencing one should never put anyone off an adventure through the Nepalese mountains (or anywhere else for that matter). We are statistically much more likely to die from being mauled by a dog in our hometown than in an earthquake. A useful statistic to remember next time you're procrastinating about going on a far-flung adventure.

Recommended Place to Stay in Gumdi

Hotel: Gumdi Hotel and Lodge
+977 9861880861
Room rate: 700 NPR (twin share).
Meal prices: 400-500 NPR

A smooth section of The Road.

Nepali road sign.

Fresh fruit on the roadside.

Taking a break...

Roadside snack shop, near Gumdi.

Day 17: Gumdi – Trishuli Bazaar

Distance: 51km

Cycling Time: 5.5hrs

Climbing: 1506m

Technical Level: 5/5

Endurance Level: 5/5

Route Summary

A tough and relentless climb on unpaved technical track for 14km. Some pushing may be required. Following this is a largely unpaved but smoother 11km undulating descent with sand sections to Bharang Bhurung, a good place to stop for lunch next to the river. Following lunch is another rough gravel climb for 4km then a fast and sweeping 13km descent to Trishuli Bazaar.

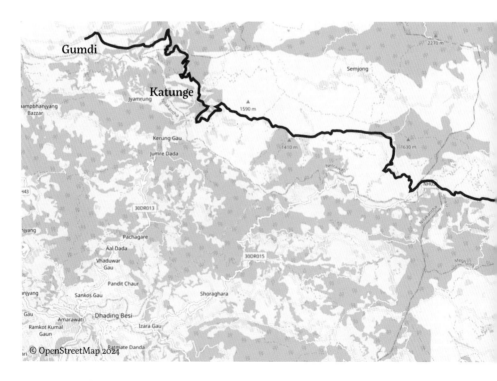

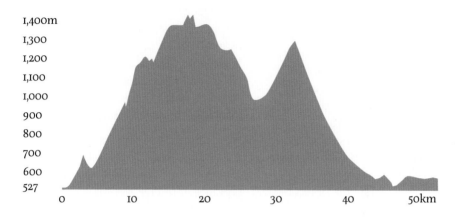

Elevation of Day 17.

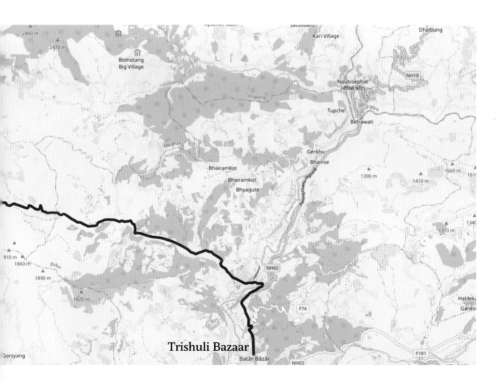

Day 17 Journal Extract

We woke in Gumdi this morning to the sound of our host lady's laugh, an amazing woman who welcomed us into her homestay last night with a huge smile, carried buckets of warm water for us to wash ourselves down and fed us the most delicious dal bhat. She was 67 and lived alone, having lost her husband to a brain tumour over 30 years ago. She explained during dinner that she has never got over the loss. She told us she keeps very busy every day because if she is idle she thinks too much and her mind becomes filled with negative thoughts, something many of us can relate to.

I remember thinking, when I first saw her warm smile on arrival from the doorstep of her quaint little homestay that she must have an idyllic life out here in the sticks. But in fact, she had been plagued by grief, day in, day out for decades. It just goes to show that we should never judge strangers or presume anything about them or their lives until they choose to inform us.

After dinner, the lady joined us for a beer and smoked a cigarette, a rare sight for a Nepali lady in the presence of foreigners. But it was her home, and she was relaxed in our company and in her skin, having been through so much.

Keeping the bikes clean is key to minimising malfunctions.

Cows crossing.

Facebook time...

She was being completely herself (always a refreshing experience when meeting others). We exchanged stories and details about our families back home, and as the night drew to a close, she pulled out her phone, logged onto Facebook, lit another cigarette and began to scroll and grin into the screen.

The next morning, she was up early, making fresh chapatis glazed with ghee, with caramelised onion and chilli scrambled eggs. The smell was amazing. As we rolled and folded the chapati around the eggs like burritos, sealing both ends, she looked on in fascination and chuckled to herself as we devoured

them. They were so good. You could taste the love.

As we packed up our things and prepared the bikes, I sensed on both sides we were all quite sad to say goodbye. We had shared some beautiful moments over a delicious couple of meals. I think we learned more from her than she did from us, despite us answering so many of her questions. As we peddled off, I reminded myself that to live a rich life we must cherish those beautiful moments; those memories are what we can hold on to as we age and wither, and that evening in the homestay with that beautiful yet grief-stricken lady were a series of short moments that I will probably never forget.

Recommended Place to Stay in Trishuli Bazaar

Hotel: Tamang Plaza +977 9741677365
Room rate: 2000 NPR (twin share).
Meal prices: 300-400 NPR

Above: Egrets taking off.

Right top: Roadside kitchen, Central Nepal.

Right: Noodle soup with all the trimmings.

Day 18: Trishuli Bazaar – Melamchi

Distance: 66km

Cycling Time: 5hrs

Climbing: 1846m

Technical Level: 3/5

Endurance Level: 4/5

Route Summary

A flowing, undulating paved route that meanders through numerous valleys for 20km before a long 24km climb to a pass at 1818m. Following this is a fun and quite technical descent through quiet forested terrain for 21km that opens up onto a wide valley floor and ends at the settlement of Bahunipati. Turn left here and ride a gentle 4km paved road to the town of Melamchi. The hotel is next to the river.

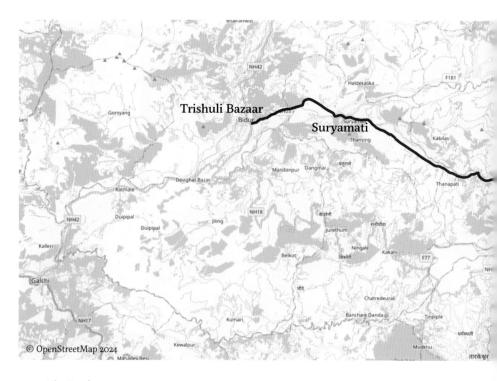

© OpenStreetMap 2024

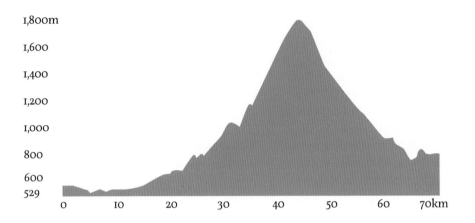

Elevation of Day 18.

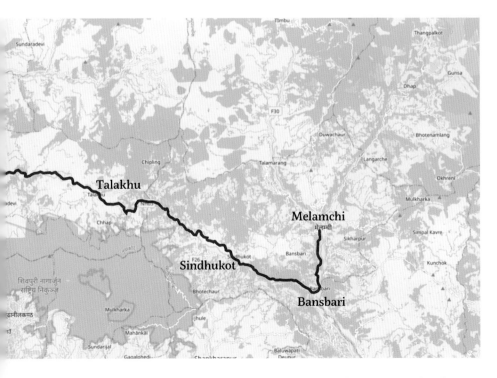

Day 18 Journal Extract

I got chatting with some locals after the ride today in the hotel restaurant – young guys, late twenties, smart and educated, speaking perfect English. I asked them how life was for them in Nepal today. I probed them about the endless complaints of political and economic squeezing and inaction on the part of the government that you hear as you travel around the country, and they concurred with it at all levels. The most startling thing about their discourse was their sense of resignation to the situation.

They complained about all sorts – empty government promises of investing in infrastructure, young people not having their voices heard, and especially the 200% tax on purchasing a car in Nepal (it was not the first time I'd heard people incredulous to this seemingly insane car tax).

I asked them why young people don't rise up and revolt against such policies. They replied swiftly that it's a waste of time. They said they don't want to waste their lives 'running into brick walls' – they believe they could waste their entire lives in revolt against government

Training for The Road starts early.

Giant swing, near Melamchi.

माझी गाँउ
MAJHIGAUN

Local road sign.

policy and inaction, but nothing will ever change. This surprised me for such dynamic, educated and energetic young men. They said most of their educated peers look to move overseas to start a new life. Australia, the UK and the US, mostly. I found this apparent brain drain on the country quite sad, given everything Nepal has to offer. I told them this, but they retorted that the remittance industry is flourishing.

In 2022 alone, remittances clocked in at over 9 billion USD, with an average 5% increase year on year since the end of the pandemic. People are happy to work overseas and those at home are happy to receive the remittances and invest back into Nepal's economy. Things in Nepal seem to be running OK under this system, they said. I couldn't really argue with that.

Recommended Place to Stay in Melamchi

Hotel: Hotel Melamchi Café Inn +977 9818371331
Room rate: 2500 NPR (twin share).
Meal prices: 300-400 NPR

Above: Maize drying.
Left top: Terraced housing in the Mid Hills.
Left: The Land of Smiles.

Day 19: Melamchi – Kartike Deurali

Distance: 62km

Cycling Time: 5.5hrs

Climbing: 1527m

Technical Level: 2/5

Endurance Level: 3/5

Route Summary

A short climb, followed by a fast paved route that meanders along a wide river valley for 31km; really pleasant and fun. This is followed by a tough 1000m, 15km climb to the settlement of Taar.

From there is a long and thrilling, semi-technical descent to the town of Kartike Deurali. A good place for lunch is the Hill Taar resort in Taar, which has great views over a spectacular valley.

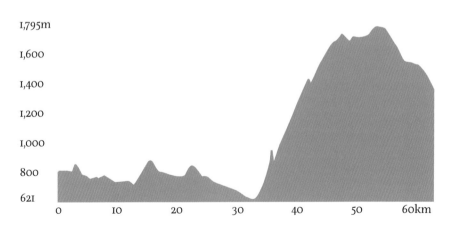

Elevation of Day 19.

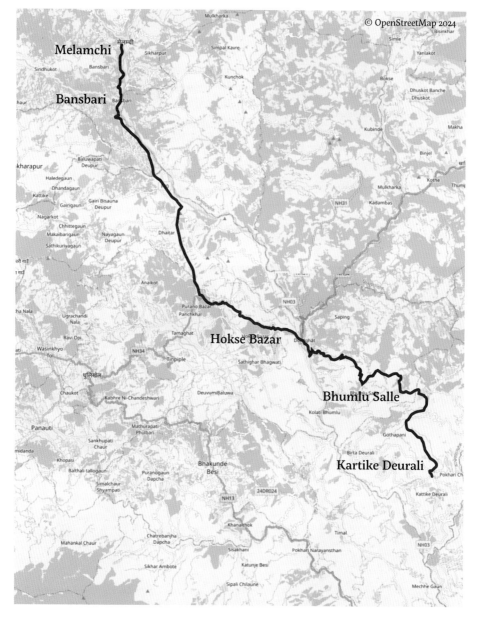

© OpenStreetMap 2024

Day 19 Journal Extract

The days are beginning to take their toll on the legs now, so Mark, Om and I ordered some extra beers this evening for anaesthetic and shared them with Sonam, our driver, and Anant, our photographer. The extra lubricant loosened our tongues, and before long we were on to a hot topic in these parts – the existence of the Yeti. I love these discussions, as I desperately want the Yeti to be real. Whenever I go home from a trip to Nepal, my youngest son always asks me if I saw the Yeti, and I always disappoint him by saying no. But I do tell him that I met a man who had seen the mythical creature, which is always an honest response. This evening, Sonam, who comes from Upper Mustang, an ancient kingdom high up on the Tibetan plateau, told us a story tonight of his cousin, some kind of herder or shepherd, who believed he experienced a yeti one dark night, and even had some grainy phone video footage to prove it. Sonam had seen the footage and swears it was authentic. He said it resembled a big bear, like 'Baloo from Jungle Book.' I asked him if it could have actually been a bear, but he said bears are not as agile on two feet as the creature in the video. 'I think the yeti is real,' he said, with wide,

glazed, convincing eyes that sent a shiver up my spine in the dank and dimly lit dining room.

Then Om began to speak about other Himalayan 'demons' – Banjhakri and Banjhakrini – shamanic deities, male and female, or possibly different aspects of the same being. They are said to be more humanoid in form and can change into non-human form to kidnap young boys and train them in the dark arts of shamanism. There have apparently been many instances of young men and boys disappearing across Nepal and Sikkim in India over the centuries, apparently having been abducted by a Banjhakri.

Above: Kaleidoscopic umbrellas; egret over the rice.

Left: Local man, Melamchi; working in the rice fields, near Melamchi.

Om said that while growing up in the countryside north of Pokhara there were numerous legends of night sightings of Banjhakri around midnight, often mounted on a horse, the rear of the animal blazing hot flames, galloping across the land.

The image of this in my head was sensational. And, just like Sonam, Om told the tale with such conviction and belief that I felt the skin tingling on the back of my head.

Recommended Place to Stay in Kartike Deurali

Hotel: Waiba Hotel +977 9841520759
Room rate: 1000 NPR (twin share).
Meal prices: 400-500 NPR

Left: The Mid Hills at Dusk.

Day 20: Kartike Deurali – Khurkot

Distance: 60km

Cycling Time: 3.5hrs

Climbing: 685m

Technical Level: 4/5

Endurance Level: 2/5

Route Summary

An exciting 8km descent on easy, unpaved tracks to start the day, followed by a mix of paved road and jeep tracks for 17km until you hit the highway at Kusheshwor (lots of lunch options here).

The highway can be quite busy, so ride with caution, but is fully paved and fluid all the way to the small town of Khurkot. Look out for the glittering wall of highway mirrors that are offered up to the goddess Seti Devi Mata as prayers to avoid accidents on this notoriously dangerous stretch of road.

Note: This road, the Sindhuli Highway, was Nepal's first properly engineered road and was designed and funded by the Government of Japan. The road is not wide enough for large trucks and only sports

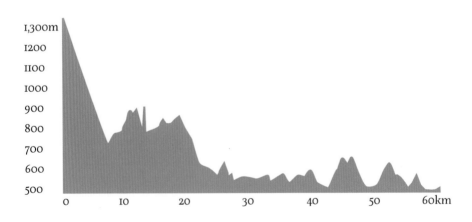

Elevation of Day 20.

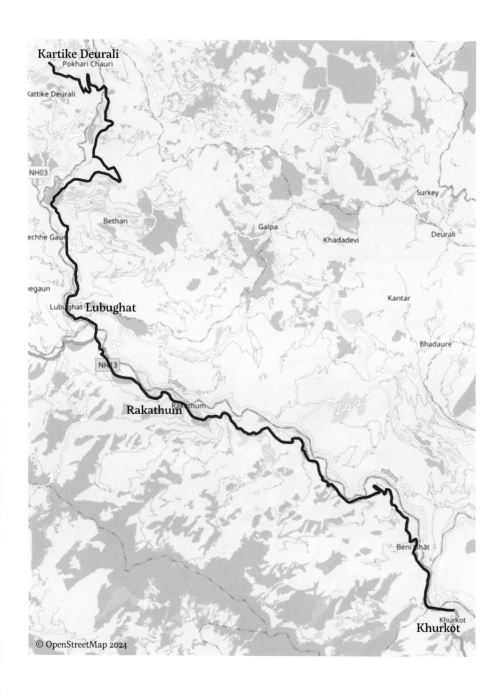

local short-haul buses, but what you need to be mindful of is the faster moving, dangerous driving of Micro buses and Sumo Jeeps which ferry people from district to district.

Day 20 Journal Extract

It was, comparatively, an uneventful day today, riding on a busyish highway, until we were startled by a glittering series of walls dripping with thousands of mirrors ahead of us. The mirrors have been put up over the years as blessings to avoid accidents, as many lives have been lost on this treacherous stretch of highway. There are terrifying drop-offs to the valley floor below from this carved out high mountain road. The mirror walls have become somewhat of a destination now, with a small temple/shop nearby selling additional mirrors to any travellers that may wish to place their own blessing. To be honest, given the intense reflections from the mirrors, especially when the sun hangs overhead, and the number of cars pulling up on the roadside to place more mirrors, the commotion on this perilous stretch seems even more treacherous as a result, so I was happy to pay my respects quickly and then peddle off into a safe zone.

Below: Memorial mirrors, near Khurkot.

Maize drying on the veranda.

Spreading the rice to dry.

Road travel in Nepal is always an experience. It's not for the faint-hearted, but if you travel with a driver who understands western driving sensibilities, and values life, there is actually very little to worry about, as speeds are rarely very high due to the poor road conditions all over the country. For example, the 'highway' linking the two main cities, Kathmandu and Pokhara, is in a terrible state, constantly under a state of construction. Just last week (Nov. 2023) we took this highway to begin the recce for the second section of The Road. It's a 200km stretch between the two cities and it took us 10 hours. But it was fun, we had lots of tea stops and met some interesting characters along the way. Never a dull moment.

The busy highways in Nepal are often like moving carnivals... polluted Mardi Gras of loud and vibrantly coloured vehicles, bouncing and shaking their way through the veins of the country like kaleidoscopic blood cells, carried by lingering clouds of exhaust fumes and dust, ferrying all manner of goods and supplies to all corners of the country, keeping the place alive and kicking. And all seemingly powered by the grunt of the horn, blasting their way up and over the undulating mountain roads, always

reaching their destinations, at some point. Not much anxiety is lost on lateness in road travel in Nepal.

In terms of road rules, I've only noticed one consistent highway rule – size matters. The bigger your vehicle, the less chance you have of having to find reverse and to go through the inconvenience of turning your neck. Just keep on truckin' and the path will magically clear ahead of you. If you have a small car on a highway, be submissive and dodge your way through, or risk getting squished.

This is why I love travelling by bicycle in Nepal, it's often just as fast as car travel, and far more fun, and your destiny is firmly in your own hands.

Recommended Place to Stay in Khurkot

Hotel: Hotel Shree Kunja
+977 9844229181
Room rate: 1500 NPR (twin share).
Meal prices: 200-300 NPR

Left: A clear day on The Road, heading east.

Morning valley mist around Khurkot.

Day 21: Khurkot – Ghurmi

Distance: 60.5km

Cycling Time: 4hrs

Climbing: 1064m

Technical Level: 2/5

Endurance Level: 3/5

Route Summary

A comfortable ride on a quiet paved highway, super fun and undulating, with small hills and descents and some small sections of unpaved track.

This section of road follows the Sunkosi – the River of Gold (*sun* in Nepali means gold, and *kosi* is river). Along the route on the other side is a town called Harkapur, which is named after one of the most famous and dangerous rapids on the river. The river is one of Nepal's most popular for long rafting trips.

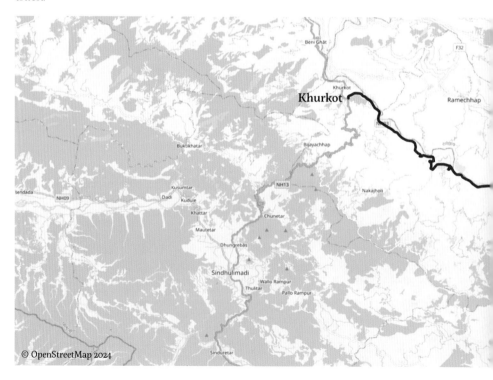

© OpenStreetMap 2024

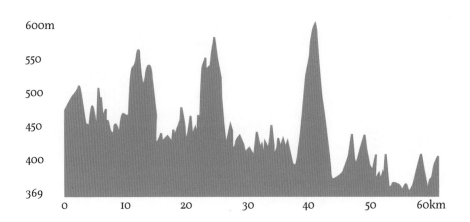

Elevation of Day 21.

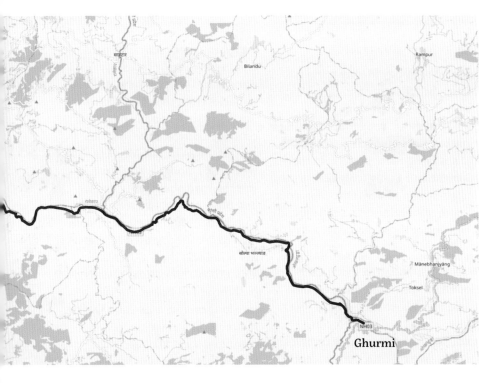

Day 21 Journal Extract

In my day-to-day life my mind is often adrift, floating and fantasising about the next best thing to do, planning ahead, sometimes wishing time to pass. I often curse myself for not being more present, in the moment. But I only truly realise this malaise when I have those moments of pure mindfulness and clarity, and I had one of those moments today.

In the crisp, sparkling morning we hit an undulating road that flowed for miles and miles on the bank, high above the Sunkosi River. The road was fast with shallow undulations but was quite technical in parts. We got into a groove, each locked into our optimum speeds and began to truly focus. My wandering thoughts retracted like tentacles from their lazy drift, back into their shell and my mind was centred, fizzing for the first time in a while. I was In The Moment. As we hurtled along, my only concern was the road ahead, anticipating and pre-empting, two steps ahead, a path that could ensure a smooth passage on the unpaved sections. My mind was there with me for about forty minutes, its pistons bashing at full power. For this rare long moment, nothing else mattered. When we stopped to regroup it took a few seconds for me to gather myself.

I took a long swallow from my water bottle and felt my head was lighter, like a spring breeze had whipped through it and blown away the cobwebs. I tingled with clarity as we re-mounted our bikes and continued along the trail.

Recommended Place to Stay in Ghurmi

Hotel: Okhadhunge Sangita Hotel
+977 9808139537
Room rate: 500 NPR (twin share).
Meal prices: 250-350 NPR

Left: Hindu pilgrims.
Right and below: Hindu rituals at dusk.

Day 22: Ghurmi – Halesi

Distance: 45.8km

Cycling Time: 3.5hrs

Climbing: 1775m

Technical Level: 2/5

Endurance Level: 4/5

Route Summary

Up, up, up, starting with a smooth paved highway that narrows to a single road. The road towards Halesi is mostly paved and cut out of the mountain, with spectacular views of the gaping valleys below. Don't ride too close to the edge as the drop offs are sheer.

Day 22 Journal Extract

I had a funny feeling in my bones while cycling up to the hill town of Halesi. I'd heard it was one of the most important spiritual centres in the country for both Hindus and Buddhists, so I was looking forward to some kind of divine experience after the long, hard slog to pedal up there. The road began as a smooth paved highway, then

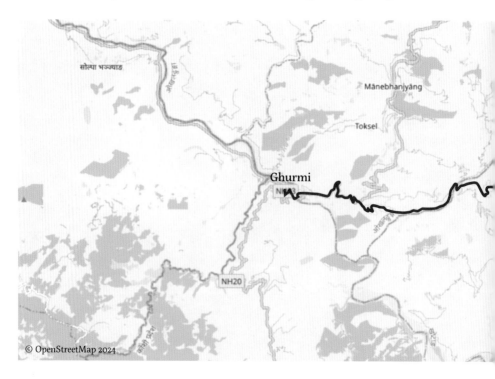

© OpenStreetMap 2024

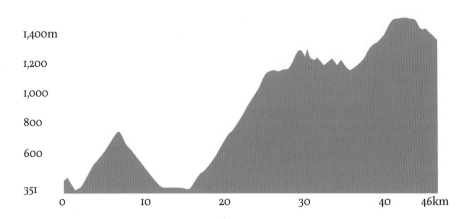

Elevation of Day 22.

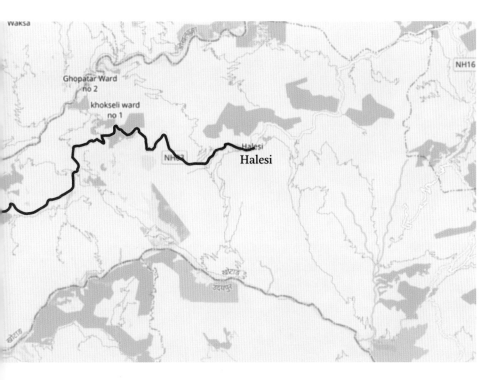

steadily narrowed to a single lane, still paved, and meandered up the side of a sheer mountainside with spectacular views through many of the distant valleys. The location for the settlement had clearly been chosen for its protected and precarious location perched high in the Himalayan foothills.

We arrived just before sundown, and immediately sensed a special aura in this ancient little town. After a quick shower, we followed the rhythmic sounds of drums through the old candle lit cobbled streets towards its spiritual heart. At its centre stood a Hindu temple on one side of the small square and a Buddhist monastery on the other. Directly behind both was a gaping cave entrance where, inside, it is believed the Hindu god Shiva once dwelled. The town was awash with excited pilgrims from both religions/philosophies from all over Nepal and neighbouring Sikkim. As darkness set in, a Hindu priest appeared, covered in orange robes with a shaved head and a pleated ponytail, swinging a thurible of pungent incense and began to conduct a ceremony. The gathering crowd swelled around him, creating a natural amphitheatre under the glow of candles and flames. It was hard not to get swept up in the ethereal and hypnotic proceedings,

Horn playing at morning prayer, Halesi.

One of many open valleys, heading east.

Ritual prayer bells, Halesi.

and when it finished, I have to say, my mind felt like a fresh wind had swept through it and I went to bed and slept like a baby.

The next morning, we woke early to go and see the morning prayers in the Buddhist monastery. We were warmly welcomed in by a kind monk and did our best to remain discreet during the long prayer service. We sat down on some soft cushions, cross-legged and began to enjoy the hypnotic chanting and spine-tingling horn playing – a sound that, to me, typifies the aura of the mystical Himalayan mountains.

A couple of the younger monks were distracted by our presence and gave us silly grins, but it wasn't a problem for the older monks. They all seemed to radiate kindness. Buddhist prayer services are always very relaxed and welcoming, and we pedalled out of this special little town an hour later feeling our souls had been nourished.

Recommended Place to Stay in Halesi

Hotel: Halesi Village Hotel
+977 036410049
Room rate: 2000 NPR (twin share).
Meal prices: 350-450 NPR

Above: Souvenir stand, Halesi.
Right: Buddhist horn playing, Halesi.

The road out of Halesi.

Day 23: Halesi – Diktel Bazaar

Distance: 35km

Cycling Time: 3hrs

Climbing: 1115m

Technical Level: 1/5

Endurance Level: 3/5

Route Summary

A long, meandering climb on paved road up over some beautiful, quiet ridges with spectacular views. From around 14km you can see Mount Everest and Mount Makalu in the distance. The climb continues, and at the 24km point you begin to descent to the beautiful bazaar town

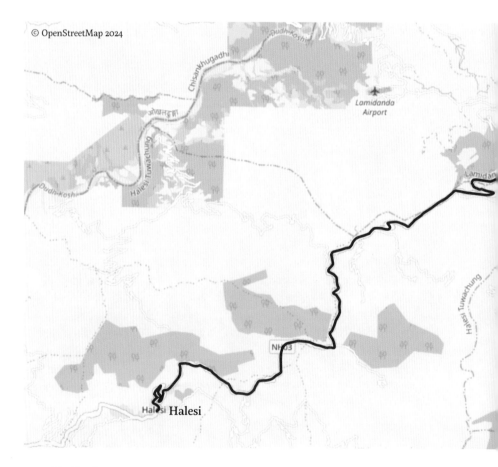

© OpenStreetMap 2024

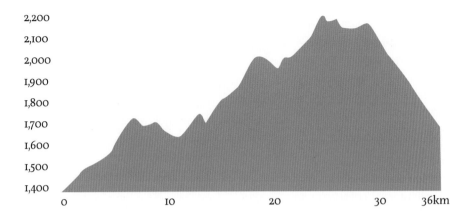

Elevation of Day 23.

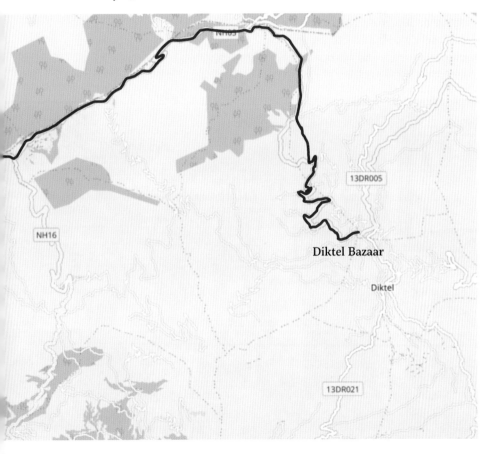

of Diktel, set on a ridge surrounded by gaping valleys. Well worth a wander around for an hour or two. The hotel is on the left side of the road going out of the town, 100m below the town gateway on the left side above a motorcycle dealer.

Day 23 Journal Extract

As you head out towards east Nepal, you notice a marked shift in the architecture of the towns and settlements as you ride through them. They become a lot more vibrant in colour, with more creative architecture. Many houses have lovely wooden balconies and window features, and Mark and I noticed for the first time the use of pot plants around people's houses for decorative purposes.

The settlement of Diktel was one of the most pleasant surprises of the trip. An idyllic little town surrounded by beautiful smoky mountains with a single high street, lined with some of the most exquisite and colourful houses and shops I'd seen on The Road. It reminded me in some way of a small, vibrantly coloured town in Mexico called San Cristobel de las Casas.

Below: Diktel high street.
Right: Diktel flags.

Back out on The Road.

The brightness of the civic pride reflected the mindset of the people, and Diktel's townsfolk were colourful characters and the children seemed to live very free lives in and around the streets and mountains.

I decided Diktel would be a good place to get a haircut, so I found a tidy little barber's shop on the high street. I asked the barber why this town was seemingly so affluent and positive. He told me it was because it was populated largely by the enterprising Rai and Limbu people of the east who have capitalised on the region's fertile land and created a rich cultural heritage in the wider Khotang district over the centuries. Diktel has historically also produced a significant number of Gurkha soldiers and many of the town's men work overseas, predominantly in the Gulf states, so remittance income is high.

After the haircut I met up with Mark for a coffee in the Cosy Coffee Shop, just down the street. It was cosy, and the coffee was relatively good.

Below: Ringing the prayer bells, Halesi.

It was lovely to see kids everywhere, ducking and diving in and out of shops as nightfall approached and the town began to sparkle under its soft, celestial lighting.

Recommended Place to Stay in Diktel Bazaar

Hotel: Suryodaya Hotel & Lodge
Room rate: 1500 NPR (twin share).
Meal prices: 250-350 NPR

Above: Pretty pot plants, a common sight in East Nepal.

Right: The next generation for The Road.

Day 24: Diktel Bazaar – Bhojpur

Distance: 87km

Cycling Time: 5.5hrs

Climbing: 2111m

Technical Level: 1/5

Endurance Level: 5/5

Route Summary

A big day. Beginning with a joyful, meandering descent for 27km, followed by a paved, but tough, 18km climb to a pass at 2360m. At the pass, views can be had of Everest, Kanchenjunga and Makalu – a good spot for lunch in this high, barren landscape. Following lunch is a thrilling 22km descent on paved road, fast and fun, just watch out for the tight hairpin bends. At the bottom of the valley begins another long, but steady, 20km climb on paved road to the town of Bhojpur.

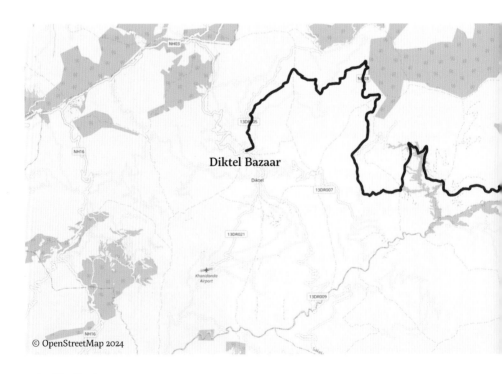

© OpenStreetMap 2024

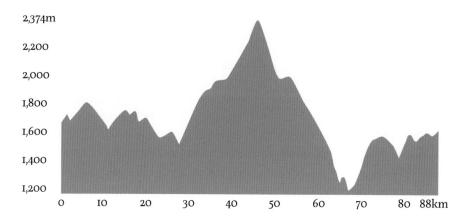

Elevation of Day 24.

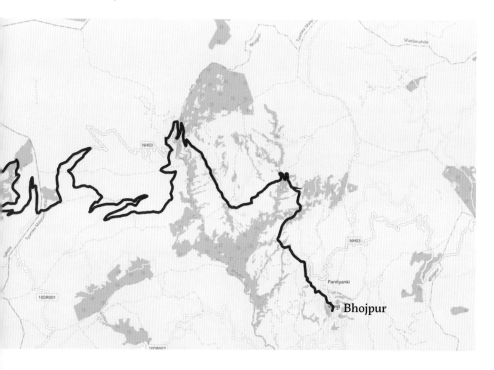

Day 24 Journal Extract

Today was a tough one, one of the toughest on the journey of The Road. The first climb of the day seemed to go on forever (for 18km), but we were (kind of) promised spectacular views of Everest, Kanchenjunga and Makalu on arrival at the pass. The images flashing through in my head of us reaching the pass to be greeted by three of the world's highest mountains spurred me on, but we had to dig deep for the last couple of kilometres.

As we came over the brow of the final hill, the sky was a bright, bright blue. We cast our eyes into the northern skies and there before us was a thick seam of cloud, draped like cotton wool over the trio of mountains, protecting them for our prying eyes. We were gutted.

We ordered some noodle soup from one of the vendors and decided to sit it out for an hour to see if the clouds would budge, but they didn't. I had seen Everest from a plane window on a number of occasions, but I was desperate to see it for real, across the Himalayan sky. I guess it just wasn't meant to be.

Our disappointment dissipated swiftly during the thrilling 22km descent to the distant valley floor below. It was a fast, paved,

One of the higher passes on The Road, but still only 2374m high.

Tracking east.

Rural home, East Nepal.

snaking road of switchbacks and tight hairpins bends that had us whooping and hollering like mad men in the warm, sun-soaked afternoon. You win some, you lose some, I thought, as we reached the bottom of the valley and crossed the bridge, and then realised we had another 20km climb to our destination of Bhojpur. These are the days you remember.

Recommended Place to Stay in Bhojpur

Hotel: Binduna Hotel
+977 9852084555
Room rate: 2000 NPR (twin share).
Meal prices: 400-500 NPR

East Nepali kitchen.

Om enjoying a tongba.

Beers around the fire
after a long day.

East Nepal architecture.

Day 25: Bhojpur – Jarayotar

Distance: 62km

Cycling Time: 4.5hrs

Climbing: 1149m

Technical Level: 2/5

Endurance Level: 3/5

Route Summary

After a tough 1km climb out of the town, there's a steady, meandering climb on paved road for 18km to the settlement of Buddha Chowk, where there is a golden Buddha statue on the right-hand side of the road. There is an option here to divert to a well-known look-out point to see Everest, Makalu and Kanchenjunga. It's a tough 2km technical climb to the viewpoint. Following this is a pleasant 19km paved descent through very rural and peaceful countryside, then a 6km low-gradient climb. The day finishes with a stunning 16km descent to the settlement of Jarayotar with open views and a Mediterranean landscape feel.

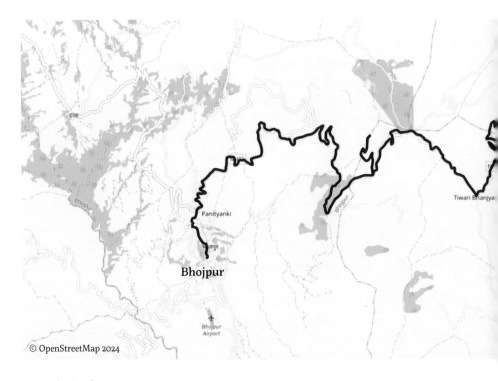

© OpenStreetMap 2024

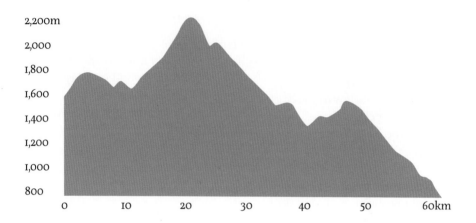

Elevation of Day 25.

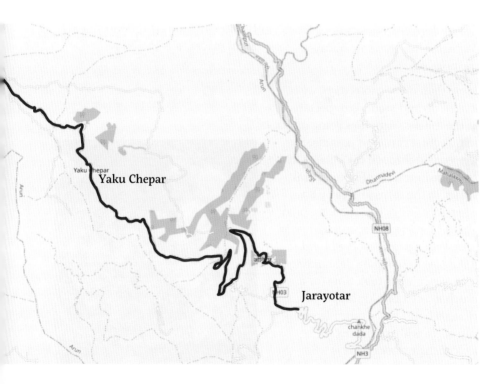

Yaku Chepar

Jarayotar

Day 25 Journal Extract

The bulk of today's ride was a gentle and pleasant meander uphill through miles of lush and fertile pastures on a single-track paved road – the most peaceful day so far.

A chorus of cicadas surrounded us for much of the day, and we regularly heard the flow of fresh mountain water through the jagged valleys, a tonic for our senses. Noticeably, there were hardly any vehicles. After 10 long days on the bikes, we seemed to naturally slow down and take our time today. As usual, we all rode at our own pace, so there were long moments when we broke up and were all completely alone, riding in the heart of this peaceful, green, mountainous land. Moments like these are always memorable.

More than on previous days, we looked up and around to spectate at the timeless activities going on in this quiet corner of paradise as we peddled through the villages. It reminded me a bit of home, rural Wales, in the 1970s and early 80s, when farm work was more manual and the pace in the countryside was slow. While people worked hard toiling over physically demanding jobs, they always took time for a much-needed break, stopping to chat, recharge and drink a leisurely cup of tea without having to look at their clocks. This is what we experienced today. Coming from urban Europe, this treat of a day really did feel like we had experienced a day in a land that time forgot.

That's the beauty of travel on a bicycle – you can move at speed and cover much ground in a day, much more so than on foot, and sometimes travel through places not always accessible by vehicle.

The bike really is the ultimate machine to carry you on a journey of cultural discovery.

Recommended Place to Stay in Jarayotar

Hotel: Indra Bahadur Homestay
+977 9819091144
Room rate: 500 NPR (twin share).
Meal prices: 300-400 NPR

Below: Fried pork, a delicacy mostly eaten in East Nepal.

Right: Quieter roads into the far east; chai stop.

Ladies of East Nepal.

An old chai master, near Jarayotar.

Roadside kitchen,
East Nepal.

Keeping warm in the
cold evenings.

Day 26: Jarayotar – Hile

Distance: 32km

Cycling Time: 2.5hrs

Climbing: 1732m

Technical Level: 1/5

Endurance Level: 4/5

Route Summary

An easy start to the day with a 7km meandering descent on mostly paved road though some beautiful terraced farmland. This is followed by 3km of flat, undulating road, then a steady 22km climb to the attractive hill town of Hile, where you can enjoy a well-deserved tongba (fermented millet beer, a specialty of the East Nepal region).

Day 26 Journal Extract

When I look back at all of the riding we have done over the last 26 days, the bulk of wonderful memories seem to be captured during the Golden Hour of each day – that magical period of light that appears from around 3-4pm, until the sun sets behind the mountains. This light transforms the land, the settlements and the people into a timeless Technicolor world that is so cinematic and vibrant that you just want to stop and take photos of everything you see.

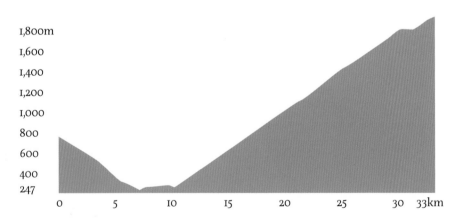

Elevation of Day 26.

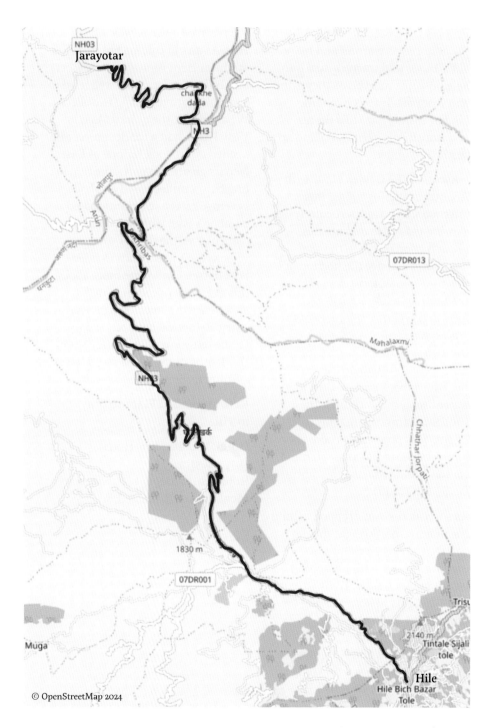

People's faces become more radiant, the land seems warmer and more alive. Buses and tractors turn into kaleidoscopic marvels as they grind and toot past. It feels like some kind of cosmic haze fills the air and transforms everything into an aesthetic wonder.

I discussed the Golden Hour with Anant, our photographer, this afternoon, as it was particularly glowing today. He told me this phenomenon is due to the sun hanging just above the horizon at this time of day, so its rays impact the Earth at a lower angle and have to travel through more of the atmosphere before they reach us. On their way to the Earth's surface, the rays encounter particles in the atmosphere, such as dust and water droplets, which filter the sunlight, ultimately making it less bright. This process also adds more indirect light to the mix, softening contours and reducing the contrasts. Fascinating stuff!

As soon as the sun dropped behind the mountains, the light quickly changed, and the cold of the evening gave us a nip, snapping us out of our Golden Hour stupor, motivating us to keep moving for the last few kilometres of riding into the picturesque mountain town of Hile. It's late November, and the nights are starting to get cold, especially at altitude.

We received a warm welcome in Hile. As an old trading hub that lies on the ancient route between Tibet and India, the locals are well used to accommodating passing travellers. We arrived at the quirky Makalu View Hotel, had a quick shower and headed out to look for one of East Nepal's greatest exports, the famous tongba – a millet-based alcoholic beverage served in an antiquated bamboo vessel with metal straps (which gives the drink its name). It looks a bit like a mini wooden beer barrel. I will write more about this evening's upcoming tongba experience in tomorrow's journal entry. Before we head out soon, I'll dig out some Alka-Seltzer from the depths of my duffle bag. I have a funny feeling I might need it.

Recommended Place to Stay in Hile

Hotel: Makalu View Hotel
+977 026540209
Room rate: 2000 NPR (twin share).
Meal prices: 350-450 NPR

Right: Local family, Hile; the famous tongba drinking vessel.

Roasting peanuts, near Hile.

Making puffed rice snacks.

Roadside party, near Hile.

Day 27: Hile – Myanglung Bazaar

Distance: 46.5km

Cycling Time: 3hrs

Climbing: 852m

Technical Level: 1/5

Endurance Level: 2/5

Route Summary

A steady climb out of town on paved road which gets steep at the 12km point for 3km. Following that is a long, meandering descent for 30km with a few small climbs, all on paved road. A fast, fun and quiet stretch of excellent paved road.

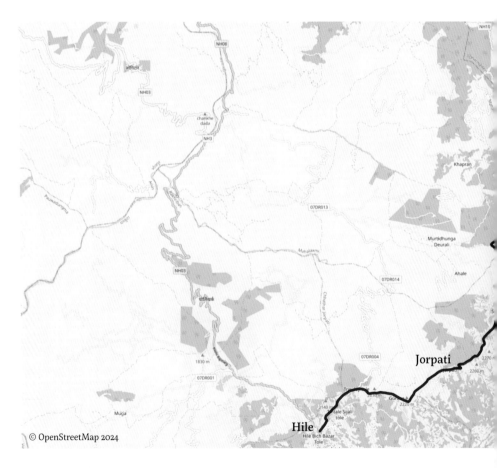

© OpenStreetMap 2024

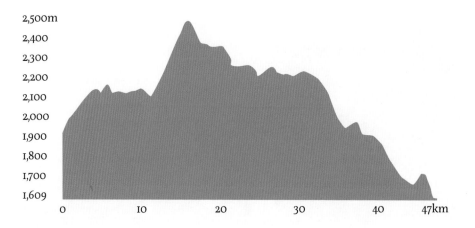

Elevation of Day 27.

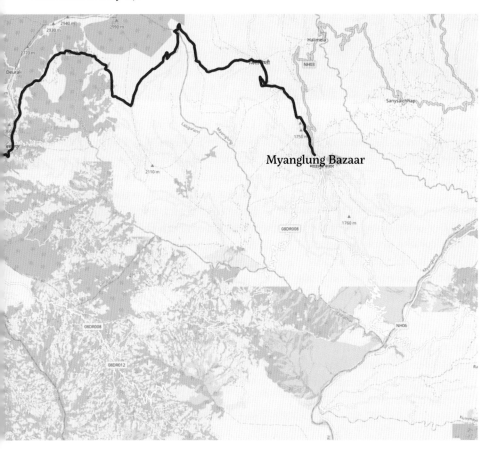

Myanglung Bazaar

A good stop for lunch is the small market town of Basantapur (the 22km point).

Day 27 Journal Extract

You know a town takes its drinking seriously when it has a 15ft statue of an alcoholic drinking vessel at its heart. In Hile, in the middle of the town's central roundabout, stands a giant tongba, with a giant metal straw sticking out of the top. There is literally no getting away from it. I imagined having a giant pint glass or a cocktail glass with a bendy straw in the centre of my hometown. Imagine.

Tongba is the drink of the Limbu people of Eastern Nepal but is by all accounts enjoyed by Tibetan people as much as Nepalis. The name tongba is attributed to the mini barrel-like vessel, but it seems the name covers both the vessel and the strange warm and cold liquid inside it. It's a millet-based drink, so the vessel is filled with copious amounts of this fermented grain – thousands of tiny crimson balls which look very much like quinoa.

Above: Hillside, near Hile.
Right top: The tongba statue, downtown Hile.
Right: Our bikes, clean and ready to go.

Looking for a warm cup of chai.

Last night, we were lucky to have a local tongba guide (one of Om's friends is from the area). He asked us if we like grilled pork. We did. He took us to one of Hile's hidden gems, a very old underground eating and drinking establishment that just served tongba and grilled pork. It was rustic to say the least – old bench tables, no heating, groups of people, particularly old men, huddled together with their hands firmly clasped around their individual tongbas, steam from the cold wafting out of their mouths as they spoke, while plates of succulent grilled pork were dropped onto the tables by the busy staff. We gobbled ours up quickly (the first pork we'd had on The Road), which was delicious, and the empty plates were swiftly replaced with steaming new ones.

As for the tongba, it had to be one of the most unusual drinking experiences I've had, and its effect was similarly atypical. The staff walked around with giant kettles of boiling water, topping up the tongbas. The boiling water filters through the millet and then rises until the chamber is full. You then leave it for a few minutes for the alcoholic millet to infuse into the water, creating a creamy liquid, which is both cold and warm when it's sucked through the metal straw. Very strange, but oddly moreish.

The taste reminded me of hay dust in the summer, that dry harvest flavour that you sometimes find in artisanal ciders. And the effect was equally strange. We each drained out tongbas three times, the recommended dosage, and headed back to our hotel for dal bhat. While the alcohol content is said to be low, between 2-5% alcohol by volume, we all felt a little woozy and spacey from the milky juice, and very relaxed. A desired effect. After dinner we enjoyed another tongba around a big open fire pit in the basement of our hotel. Yep, you read that right. No EU health and safety regulations in these parts.

I woke this morning with a thumping headache. Good job today was only going to be a relatively short ride. The Alka-Seltzer fizzed down my gullet a treat. As we peddled out of town and past the statue, we all gave a nod of respect to the giant Tongba.

Recommended Place to Stay in Myanglung Bazaar

Hotel: Blue Heaven Hotel: +977 02640168
Room rate: 2000 NPR (twin share).
Meal prices: 550 NPR

Below: Local chef, Myanglung Bazaar; local fruit and vegetables.

Day 28: Myanglung Bazaar – Sankranti Bazaar

Distance: 56km

Cycling Time: 5hrs

Climbing: 2397m

Technical Level: 5/5

Endurance Level: 5/5

A tough day. Carry plenty of fluids and snacks for the big, unpaved, remote climb and descent.

Route Summary

A tough day. Carry plenty of fluids and snacks for the big, unpaved, remote climb and descent. After starting with a fast descent on paved road for 10km, there is a tough, unpaved 16km (900m) climb, then quite a technical 14km descent until you hit an asphalt road. From here it's paved, but quite steep, for the final 15km climb to the quaint settlement of Sankranti.

Day 28 Journal Extract

The penultimate day of riding. Fourteen days down, just two to go. The end is in sight, so we have dropped our guards a bit the past few days, enjoying one too many tongbas and a couple of extra beers and late nights. All bad ideas in hindsight. 'It ain't over till the fat lady sings', and the Queen Stage of Section 2 of The Road lay ahead of us today.

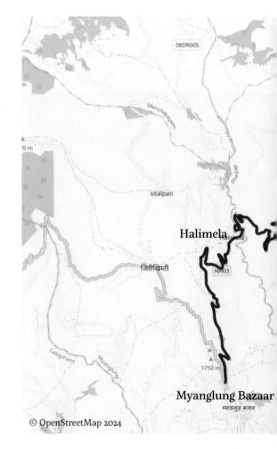

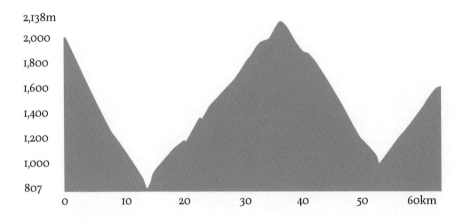

Elevation of Day 28.

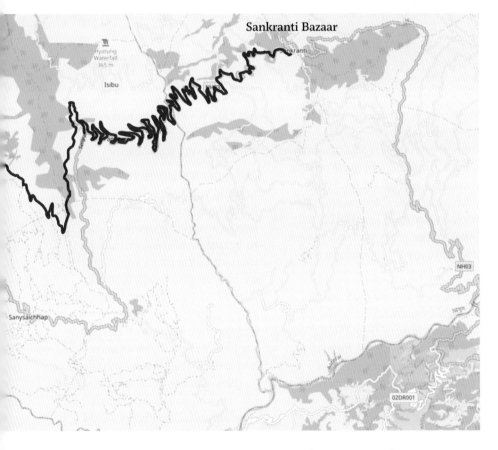

With almost 2400m of climbing, we knew it would be a tough day, but more than half of it was up and over a huge, unpaved and quite remote mountain we did not anticipate, with some super steep sections, so we took our time, and walked our bikes on the rocky parts and I went deep into my thoughts for a few long moments.

It's not easy to look back and remember each day individually. It's a good job I've been taking lots of notes, otherwise the memories would have all gelled into one long beautiful blur. Reminiscing on the events of the past two weeks were interspersed with pining to see my kids, who I'll have been away from for three weeks in total, a long stretch by any standards.

The fondest memories that came to mind were not so much of the fabulous riding, which has just been a joy on this never-ending rollercoaster of road; instead, I thought of the many communities we have stopped with, to drink chai, raksi, or chang, and exchange stories about where we come from, our families, our jobs, and why we are here. Several farmers we met had sent their kids to university in Kathmandu in search of a better life. They were super proud that their sons and daughters would soon be engineers or teachers. Doing their best to ensure a better life for the next generation was their raison d'être, which gave them purpose and motivation to continue their daily toil out on the land. It's something we all strive for in our own individual ways as parents. We really are all just the same.

There has also been a lot of rice harvesting going on during the trip, with big threshing machines similar to ones used for corn in Europe many years ago that you often see during vintage demonstrations in the regional agricultural shows in Britain in the summertime. This brought back fond memories of my childhood, seeing all the community working together to bring in the harvest, enjoying regular chang breaks in the same way we used to look forward to our cider breaks.

One of the most lucid memories from the past days that came to mind, as I heaved my bike up that steep, steep hill, was from a hilly settlement we had stopped at a few days previously to watch the harvest in full swing. It was all happening – villagers everywhere, a glorious commotion. They were threshing by hand, whipping the rice in bundles onto the hard ground to separate the grain from the straw, then tossing the straw onto a giant stack,

Eastern Himalayas in the distance.

where several buffalo were used (holstered around a central pole, which they lurched and lumbered around) to turn the straw and settle it down into a level stack. The farmers invited us to join and to have a go at the manual threshing. We happily accepted.

Stepping into the threshing patch, I was immediately whisked back to my childhood – the heat, the dust, the musty smell of the dry grain and husk. We were shown how to wrap the bundles using an old piece of rope, then hoist it over our shoulders and slam it down onto the ground as hard as we could to release the grains from the straw.

It took five of six lashes to release all the rice grain, then one last heave to toss the heavy straw bundle onto the stack for the approaching buffalo to settle. I only whipped this one bundle, and I was puffing a bit, and sweating. But what I remember most was that itching feeling in the join of my sweaty forearm from the dust. I attacked it with my nails, just like I used to as a kid.

We reached the top of the forested hilltop after a 16km upward slog. I snapped out of reminiscing mode and focused on the route ahead – we had 16km of quite technical downhill terrain ahead of us.

We opened up both front and back suspensions to the max, and down we went.

Recommended Place to Stay in Sankranti Bazaar

Hotel: Crazy Time Restaurant and Lodge
Room rate: 500 NPR (twin share).
Meal prices: 250-350 NPR

Left: Turning the rice straw.
Right: Limbu lady.
Below: Separating the rice.

Day 29: Sankranti Bazaar – Phidim Bazaar

Distance: 38.7km

Cycling Time: 3hrs

Climbing: 1304m

Technical Level: 2/5

Endurance Level: 2/5

Route Summary

A flowing and meandering descent for 25km with great views of the Kanchenjunga massif, dropping down into a warm, subtropical valley with lush vegetation. A good stop for lunch is the Tamor Rafting Report, just after the river crossing. From here is a steady, paved climb that twists and turns all the way up to the end of The Road at Phidim. The journey finishes on top of a small hill overlooking the town, at the statue of the goddess Palgunanda. Opposite the statue is the End of The Road bar, where you can celebrate with cold refreshments.

Day 29 Journal Extract

Our last day, and it was a fitting one. Blazing sunshine greeted us as we left the hotel and dropped immediately into a wide-open valley descent, with the Kanchenjunga massif as our backdrop – a pinch-yourself moment. We could soon feel the warm currents of air from

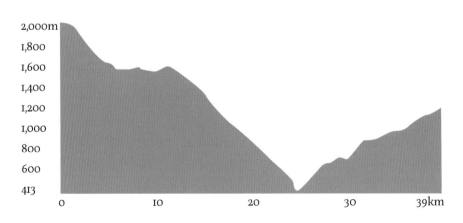

Elevation of Day 29.

Eastern Himalaya panorama.

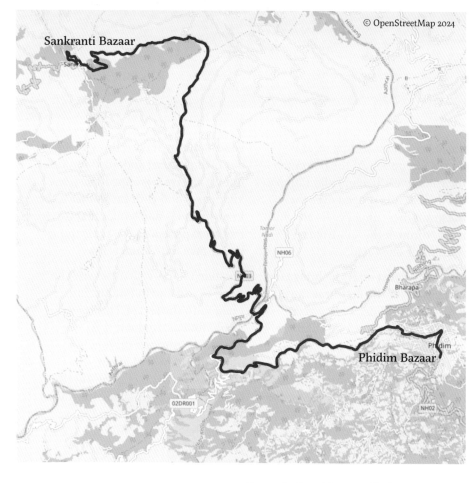

the lower land warming us as we descended into it. At the bottom of the valley were banana plantations, the thick leaves draped over the track, another thing I've loved whilst riding through the sub-tropical sections of The Road.

We stopped just after the bridge for lunch, and for the first time during the daytime riding, we enjoyed a cold beer before the final climb up to Phidim. Excitement was setting in, we were on the home straight, literally; and Mark, Om and I rode together for the final few kilometres into town. Over the course of the past 29 days, the three of us have rarely ridden together. We have

gone at our own pace, drawn into our own physical and mental zones, but we always regrouped every few kilometres and gave each other knowing nods and smiles that we had all experienced the same things in our own individual ways.

We didn't know exactly where The Road would end in Phidim, but I had faith the end of The Road would find us. And it did. As we weaved up through this quaint little mountain settlement, Om spotted some kind of shrine in the trees on a hill overlooking the town. We peddled towards it, and as we approached, a beautiful statue of a Hindu goddess revealed itself on a small little square overlooking the ramshackle tin-roofed hill town, like some kind of guardian angel. We all knew that this point was the end of The Road. We dismounted our bikes and hugged emotionally and ecstatically on the steps of the shrine as the Golden Hour of sunlight shone over us. A moment I will never forget.

We asked some locals about the statue and were told her name was Palgunanda, a goddess of wisdom. Though we were not sure how much wiser we were after traversing the country from west to east, we were certainly enlightened and humbled by the power of the human spirit

of the peoples of Nepal's Mid Hills that was consistent right the way through the 1650km journey along The Road.

Recommended Place to Stay in Phidim Bazaar

Hotel: Manaswi Hotel
+977 024523111
Room rate: 2000 NPR (twin share).
Meal prices: 350 NPR

Left: The tranquillity of East Nepal.
Below: The end of The Road, Phidim.
Pages 260-261: Limbu ceremony, Phidim.

Returning to Kathmandu

From Phidim it is a long trek back to Kathmandu. If you travel, as recommended, with a guide and jeep support, the trip takes two full days. This will all be organised by the folks at Himalayan Single Track.

If you are bike-packing and prefer to cycle out of the mountains, you can extend the trip by a couple of days and ride the beautiful road from Phidim to Illam, which takes you through some stunning tea plantations, and continue on a busy road to Bhadrapur airport, near the Indian border.

There are several daily flights from Bhadrapur to Kathmandu (approx. 100 USD single fare).

Left: Swayambhunath Temple, Kathmandu, Nepal.

INTERVIEWS

Interviews with the local game changers who have helped to shape and develop the sport of mountain biking in Nepal in recent years.

Ajay Pandit Chhetri
The Inspiration

Photo by Gauravman Sherchan.

Ajay Pandit Chhetri was born in Kathmandu into a family of shopkeepers with no interest in sport and has gone on to become the most decorated mountain biker in Nepal, with five Nepal national championship titles and five victories in the Yak Attack (the world's highest mountain race), as well as podium and high-ranking finishes in races worldwide, from India to South Africa to Costa Rica, the US, the UK and Switzerland.

Ajay is also the course record holder of the gruelling Tour of the Dragon – a 260km non-stop mountain bike race in the Bhutanese Himalaya.

Since retiring from elite completion, Ajay now focuses on his two businesses – MTB Nepal, which offers performance coaching for elite riders, as well as tailor made tours for groups of riders wishing to explore the Nepalese Himalayas, and MTB COGS, a mountain bike parts and repair business he runs with a friend.

You grew up in the city of Kathmandu. Was cycling part of your life in your early years? What memories of cycling do you have from that time?

I consider myself very lucky that I grew up in the early 90s and had the privilege to see Kathmandu pollution and crowd free. During that time Kathmandu wasn't as built up as it is now. I remember Hero cycles (from India) were used by most people to commute, as well as for shopping and fun. As there were very few vehicles in those days, bicycles were the main mode of transport in the city. My family used to own one small bicycle. My cousins and I used to take turns to ride it, but we were only allowed to once per week, on the weekend.

We were so excited and impatient for that day to arrive! The memories of the joy and freedom I had as a kid cycling the streets of Kathmandu will stay with me forever.

When did you first ride a mountain bike? Did you realise then that it was something that would potentially shape your future life and career? Or was it something that developed slowly?

I started riding a BMX in around 2002. I modified that BMX bike by adding seven rear gears and a single speed at the front. I had already started working at a bike shop and had some knowledge of bike mechanics. Around 2004, I had the chance to build a real mountain bike. I collected some old and some new parts and an old frame. I started as a junior rider with no thoughts of making it a career, as it really wasn't an option in those days, but over time I started racing and doing well, becoming National Champion in 2009. That was the time I realised my potential and decided to take it seriously and become a professional. When I won my first Yak Attack in 2010, some doors to travel and compete were opened by Phil Evans of MTB Worldwide and I started travelling to Europe for races. It was during this period that I realised I could pursue a career in mountain biking.

You have competed in some of the world's toughest cross-country mountain bike races. Which were the toughest three and why?

The first ones that come to mind as the toughest are:

1. **Cape Epic in South Africa (2012).** It's definitely the big daddy of mountain bike stage races globally. It's hot and humid, with average daily distances of 100-120km, which takes an average of four to five hours at speed in over 30-degree heat. Coming from Kathmandu, the humidity was tough! The trails are also new every year so you don't really know what to expect for the seven days. For sure the toughest race I've done.

2. **La Ruta in Costa Rica (2011).** A notoriously gruelling jungle race from the Pacific coast to the Caribbean coast of the country. Trails were rough and went up to 30% gradient. We crossed rivers, rode through mud and over landslides, hot and sticky. It's often billed as the world's toughest race, and I can say from experience it is up there.

3. **Yak Attack in Nepal.** As the world's highest mountain bike race, due to the altitude the oxygen levels become low as you ascend toward the Thorong La pass (5400m). It's hard to push yourself to the max with such thin air, despite daily

Photo by Gauravman Sherchan.

distances being quite short. Yak Attack is not just a race against competitors, but also with yourself, your mind and the more hostile side of nature.

What keeps you going mentally when your body is at its limit during a race?

Racing was always my dream, so being in a racing environment is a realisation of my dream. This is enough to motivate me to push myself to the maximum. The weather, trails and the landscapes obviously affect my mentality during each race, but I always focus on positivity, remembering my achievements and future goals. This is how I keep myself mentally strong.

List your favourite three regions to ride in Nepal and why.

It's hard to limit to just three regions! But here goes:

1. Annapurna Region, Mustang side. It's not the hidden paradise it once was, but this region still holds its beauty. The unique landscape, trails, and people have always added a special beauty. Here you can ride right in the lap of the Himalayas and that is what I love. Riding in the fresh air and big skies feels like a form of meditation.

2. Phaplu from Solukhumbu region. This region is fresh and has many virgin trails, which are still undiscovered. We had the chance to explore this region in 2020 before lockdown during our High Altitude Training Camp. The alpine forest gives European vibes and the trails are quiet. The elevation is perfect for High altitude training as well.

3. Kathmandu and Pokhara. Joint third! I could never choose between these two places. Both hold special beauty in their own ways. Around Kathmandu there are tons of trails from jeep track to single track and there is so much history all around – stupas, temples, ancient streets. It's a very special and atmospheric city. Pokhara too is a beautiful city with less pollution than Kathmandu, and staggering mountain views as you ride the assortment of trails that lead down to the lake.

Are there any Nepali regions you wish to ride, but have yet to explore on your bike?

Most of Nepal is still a hidden paradise for cycling, so it's hard to choose one. But I would love the challenge of the Great Himalayan Trail especially in the western side of Nepal, around Rara Lake and beyond, which remains quite unexplored until now.

You are going on a long ride into a remote region. What are the three most essential items you take with you in your backpack?

1. Bike parts (and knowing how to fit them!) – in rural and remote Nepal, if you have a technical problem, you will have to fix it yourself.

2. First aid kit – you will mostly be riding outside towns and villages (where some basic health provisions may exist.) So bring a good kit with a variety of items to fix you up if you have any problems.

3. Warm clothes – temperatures plummet at night in Nepal and after a hard day of riding your body will need to stay warm. Pack a good set of thermal clothing, and a beanie and gloves.

Some people are apprehensive to come to Nepal because of the high-altitude riding, remote and hard to get to locations and the treacherous roads. What, from your experience, would you say to alleviate these concerns? Is Nepal a safe place to ride?

This is a good question and I'm very happy to answer it. Firstly, most of Nepal is not high Himalaya. The southern part of the country is actually almost as low as sea level. We have riding opportunities in this region, the Terai. It's subtropical and hot in these lowlands. Then we have the Mid Hills, which are higher, 1000-2500m, which is a great altitude for riding. This is where most Nepali mountain bikers ride. It's also the most culturally rich area, so the Mid Hills are great for adventure mountain bike travel. All the back roads are safe and easy, the road quality is not great, so cars and trucks do not go too fast. Even when you go really remote everyone will be very friendly and helpful.

The roads can be quite hazardous, but that is part of the adventure! You can alleviate your concerns by travelling with a reputable guide or tour company, or renting a private jeep instead of taking public transport between big towns (like Kathmandu to Pokhara).

How is Nepalese hospitality in rural areas? Can foreigners expect a warm welcome?

Tourism in Nepal is one of our biggest industries, and for us, providing a warm welcome is very important. Even myself, I've always felt a warm welcome wherever I go in the country with my tour groups or if I'm travelling with friends. Rural areas are especially welcoming. Village people find it honourable and feel pride when a tourist is visiting and will always want to show them the best parts. So yes, a warm welcome is guaranteed!

What are the three most useful (simple) Nepali phrases to learn for a backcountry mountain bike adventure?

1. **Namaste** (hello)

2. **Yo bato kaha janxa?** (Where does this way go to?)

3. **Khana pani pauxa?** (Can we get food and water?)

Laxmi Magar
The Female Trailblazer

Photo by Bijay Thapa.

Laxmi Magar has been the standout trailblazer in female Nepali mountain biking over the past decade, enduring years of solitude as the only high-level female rider in a male-dominated sport and competing in male category races as female categories simply did not exist. Laxmi's tenacity and inspiration to others resulted in a flurry of new female riders coming onto the scene, which in turn has led to female category mountain bike races being introduced in Nepal.

Laxmi was raised in the small, isolated village of Gerkhu, 78km outside Kathmandu. The only bicycle she saw as a young child belonged to her visiting cousins. She would steal the bike for a few moments and still remembers the instant feeling of freedom and joy.

Laxmi is a seven-time national female champion, won gold at the 2019 South Asian Games and has won the gruelling Yak Attack, as well as other accolades internationally from India to Sri Lanka and Switzerland.

When Laxmi is not training for competitions, she can be found guiding mountain bike tourists in the Annapurna region and helping to develop the next generation of riders through the Nepal Cycling School.

What are your first memories of riding a bike?

I have so many memories, but I always remember the feelings of freedom, fascination and joy when I first began riding a bike when my cousins came to visit with their bicycles. I would steal their bikes and pedal away into the open spaces. Even in those early days I felt a special connection to a bike. A big memory was the first time I raced in Kakani in 2008. That was

Photo by Bijay Thapa.

extremely challenging and made me realise I had to work hard to improve.

When did you get your first mountain bike? Describe your feelings at that time.

I bought my first mountain bike in 2013 through instalments when I started working at Pathfinder bike shop. It felt super light and so much faster. It was a different feeling with equipment like suspension, which meant I could ride more challenging terrain. It opened up a whole new world for me.

When did you realise that you wanted to take mountain biking seriously and compete and make a living from it?

At Pathfinder, I had the chance to learn about mountain biking routes, itineraries and tours, which really brought me into the industry with a deep interest. It was there that I learned about MTB races in the mountains. I also stopped worrying about damaging my bike, as I could quickly get parts and fix issues at the bike shop. Then my confidence became strong to pursue racing and adventure. During national events I raced against army and police riders who were very fit. This pushed me to train harder. At the Asian Games I competed against riders from China, Japan, Korea, Thailand, Indonesia, all very fit and with good technical ability. This motivated me to further improve. I knew I could be as good as them and make a living from the sport if I worked hard. So I began working as a guide and training harder, along with carrying out my studies in fine art.

It is well known that in Nepal it is not as socially acceptable for young women to participate in sports as it is in western countries. Is this still an issue and have things improved?

Yes, it has been very challenging to be a female rider in Nepal. For a long time I raced with boys/men, as women's categories did not exist. But thankfully, this has changed in recent years, and now we have female categories in all types of races, from cross country to enduro.

How were you viewed in your family and society being the only competitive female rider for so long?

When I first started mountain biking, I think everyone thought I was from a different planet! Here was this strange girl doing this dangerous sport with only boys.

I used to miss social gatherings often because I was training, which is not normal in Nepal. But now things are different, my family and people around me respect what I do and encourage me to keep riding.

Are there any Nepali regions you wish to ride, but have yet to explore on your bike?

Yes, I would love to explore the Great Himalayan Trail.

Are the Nepali hills a safe place for women to ride?

Yes, absolutely, Nepal is safe for female riders. Personal safety is not really a concern, but it's important to remember the mountains of Nepal are challenging and intense, so visiting female riders should make sure they are fit and strong with a positive mindset before coming to ride here. Accommodation can be very basic as well in the mountains, so be prepared for that also. You are guaranteed an adventure!

Santosh Rai The King of Enduro Adventure

Photo by M. Lama.

Santosh Rai grew from humble beginnings in rural east Nepal. With a keen sense of adventure inherent from birth, Santosh's intrepid journey led him to Kathmandu as a teenager and into the whitewater rafting business. After a chance ride on a mountain bike from a fellow guide, Santosh was hooked and has since dedicated his life to mountain bike guiding and to pushing the boundaries of enduro riding discovery in some of the most remote areas of Nepal. Santosh is co-founder of Himalayan Single Track, a travel and tour company based in Kathmandu, and works in various capacities to encourage younger generations to take up the sport.

You grew up in a very rural part of Nepal. Were bicycles part of everyday life when you were a child? What is your earliest memory of cycling?

I was born in a place that was rich in nature, right in the lap of Mt Makalu and Mt Kanchenjunga. Swimming across a river each day to get to school and hiking into the jungle to pick wild mushrooms and sling-shotting *kallis* (jungle chickens) was a normal part of my everyday life. Rivers, trees, rocks, hills (not mountains, as we were still a few days walk from the Himalayas), wind, rain and sunshine was just a part of my everyday existence. Awareness of nature, living with it was just a normal part of life. Bikes were not a part of this life.

It wasn't until I travelled three days on foot to Hille, and had my first ever experience of roads and bus rides that I began to notice bikes. Down in the flat lands (Terai) region of Nepal where farmers used old steel bikes (Buddho Bikes or 'old man's bikes', as we say in Nepali).

The first bike I rode was a Buddho Bike, I was on the back with my uncle, a carpet maker, on the front.

We went too fast and crashed into barbed wire. I still have the scar!

I felt a connection with cycling, and I found a place where I could hire a bike for four rupees per hour. I rode it for hours around a flat football ground in Thali. The bike had no brakes and the pedals had fallen off just leaving the iron rods. This is how I learned to ride, on such a crappy bike.

When I began work for a rafting company, I was integrated into the adventure tourism part of Thamel. I borrowed mountain bikes from friends and rode them. My first real experience with riding a mountain bike was through a friend, Rabindra. He had a bike and we became friends while handing out rafting flyers to tourists in Thamel. I brought him bottles of Coke and momos and cajoled him into lending me his mountain bike. I was not familiar with the concept of brakes and had quite a crash and broke the bike. It was a while until Rabindra spoke to me again.

Back in those days the mountain biking community in Nepal was very small.

Describe your first experience as a mountain bike guide.

I was always an active worker, doing extra jobs and things for the more senior staff and guides in the rafting company. Hence, I became a favourite of many of the rafting guides and progressed up the ladder. It was also well known that by this time I was obsessed with mountain biking.

There was a lady from one of the rafting trips that wished to go on a bike ride, so the rafting guide recommended me as the guide. A deal was made that she would pay for my bike hire from Himalayan Mountain Bike and I would be her guide for the ride to Nagarkot, which is a 67km round trip from Kathmandu with 1,000m of climbing.

Me! Raw from the village, no idea where Nagarkot was, terrified of speaking English, with limited experience on a bike and incredibly excited. The idea of saying no was not in my makeup.

I had an uncle that lived in Thali, it was kind of on the way to Nagarkot so that was the direction I headed off in.

My idea of guiding was that if she booked a trip and rode behind me at a steady pace, she would be happy. The thought of actually talking to the client or the idea of her asking me a question was terrifying, so on the ride, every time she came close to me, I rode away, time and time again. This comical scenario led to me riding at a frantic pace. Every time I got ahead, I would ask locals for directions and stuff any food I could find into my mouth. I also had this idea that if I was happy and smiling and laughing, she would be happy. So there I was, this moronic, dumb, laughing kid dragging an exhausted lady up to Nagarkot and back! It goes without saying that she was furious with me and complained to my boss. She stopped at Bouldnath, booked a hotel and literally collapsed.

Which discipline of mountain biking do you prefer?

First it's enduro and all mountain riding, as it's fun and lets you play with your skills. Second it's XC riding, as you get to go on a journey and see amazing places.

Describe a typical day during one of your mountain bike tours.

First thing in the morning is coffee... it's always coffee. I like to wake up and go outside and get a feel for the weather, check the bikes and check in with the driver or porters before meeting up with the clients.

I don't often like to eat breakfast, it's not a habit I have developed. Breakfast is not a common thing in Nepal. This means I always carry extra food, so I don't get hungry. My bag always has snacks in it, and I like to collect local items and fruit as we pass through villages.

Once the bikes have been checked I head to the breakfast table to make sure the clients have everything they need and let the clients know what time we plan to leave.

I arrange the packing of anything that needs to go with the porters and then manage the bills for the teahouse, check the budget and finally pack my own gear. I always spend time talking to the hotel/ teahouse owners and staff and have some fun with them. It's important as these people can be called on for help or favours in times of need. Good local relationships are priceless in the remote regions.

Then we ride. Riding days mostly follow a plan, but it depends on the clients. Some are adventurous so we can sometimes go and explore other trails and single tracks. After lunch, we continue riding.

On reaching the destination for the day, I go and see the teahouse team and make sure rooms are ready and some snacks and tea is coming for the clients.

I do a quick assessment of the bikes to see if anything needs fixing and use the help of the drivers or porters to clean them up and put them in a secure place, then I brief the clients on the areas they can explore or wander around the village. I also make sure the clients order their dinner, as in teahouses hot meals can take a long time to cook. At this point we talk about the PFT = Plan For Tomorrow.

Once everyone is back in the teahouse, safe, warm and drinking tea or beer, happy and telling the stories of the day, I consider my mission complete.

You are well known for your adventurous spirit. How do you define adventure?

When I arrived in Thamel, the tourist zone of Kathmandu, it was incredulous to me, having grown up in remote Eastern Nepal, that there were these people (I found out later the word for them was tourists) from all over the world who came here to explore and PAY FOR adventures. Things like swimming and rafting in rivers, walking up hills and in jungles, things that, until I left my village, were part of my normal life, part of what I thought was normal for everyone. It seems they had a tag word for these activities and that word was Adventures.

It felt so natural to me after my upbringing that I should be a part of this tourism adventure 'scene'. Early on I conceptualised the idea that adventure is the 'KEY' that sparks the ignition of life. I was born into adventure, therefore I think I live it differently than others.

If I had to define it, adventure is a never-ending journey, and that journey could be in anything – nature, art, sports, travel...it depends on you as a person and your life experiences.

It's also an addiction, whatever you learn from one adventure you always want to learn more, do more. The more you learn the further you can go and the closer to the edge you can get.

In tourism terms, Adventure also has a lot to do with timing, situation and luck. Elements and Nature can turn something normal into a fabulous adventure.

But as a guide, ultimately the true adventure is living to tell the story, returning home with your clients having taken them close to the edge, not over it, or so close that fear takes over, but just enough.

How to accomplish that is learnt and developed over time through experience. The feeling of going to the edge, in simple terms, is something like when you are really hungry, and somebody brings you a delicious meal. That feeling is the best and you are so happy to be eating it, that the journey to the meal, all the hard and terrifying bits of hunger are forgotten, and just the good memory of the meal remains. Adventure is ingrained in me. It's really quite hard to put into words.

Do you try to take your clients to the edge of their limits? Or do you let them choose the pace of the adventure?

It depends on the clients. Some clients are loose and seek and crave adventure and wish to push the limits. I like to give them some freedom to do this, but I always keep a constant awareness of our location and the risks involved.

Other clients need to have their limits pushed by gentle coaxing. I guess in both cases I am controlling them. In the first case making sure it's safe and in the second case encouraging the clients to push the limits a bit.

What is your favourite region to ride in Nepal and why?

For riding trails my favourite place is Phaplu in the lower Everest Region, because of the trails. For giving the clients a great single-track riding experience my favourite place is also Phaplu/Pikey Peak in the lower Everest Region.

For showing clients culture, experiences and breathtaking landscapes then it is Upper Mustang. For most clients it is an out of this world experience.

As the owner of a mountain biking tour company, do you spend a lot of time looking for new trails? Are there any new

Photo by M. Lama.

areas or regions of the country in the process of opening up to mountain biking?

Yes, I spend a lot of time exploring new trails. I do this mostly in the off-season.

East Nepal has the potential to become Nepal's next big mountain biking destination. There is a lot of variation to the trials, good road access and many small local bike clubs starting to expand the trail networks.

Are there any areas of the country you have yet to experience on your mountain bike, but wish to?

The Dolpa area, both Upper and Lower.

Usha Khanal Taking Female Riding to the Next Level

Usha Khanal is one of the rising stars in Ladies Mountain biking in Nepal. From humble beginnings in the Western Hills, Usha has worked and studied in a wide range of areas on her quest to achieve a livelihood from sport, which is not an easy task in a country like Nepal, least of all for a young woman. Today Usha is a professional mountain bike guide as well as the Number I female elite cross-country rider in Nepal and has represented her country at the South Asian Games and at the UCI Cycling World Championships in Scotland.

When did you receive/buy your first mountain bike? What were your emotions at that time?

I bought my very first bicycle in the year 2015 – it was a Giant XTC bicycle (Sky blue and White). I immediately loved that bike as they were my favourite colours. But I had to hide it from my family for almost a week. They were shocked and scolded me for spending that money on a silly bicycle, especially as the school I worked in had recently closed due to the earthquake. All I could do was listen to them. But I felt so lucky – I felt like I was flying in the sky with joy – having a bike of my own gave me so much happiness.

When did you realise that you wanted to take mountain biking seriously and compete?

I started mountain biking around the year 2014. But I never took it seriously until 2017 when a documentary movie was made on myself and two other Nepalese female mountain bikers. I realised after watching it I could achieve a much higher level if I worked hard. I started working as a mountain bike guide but never took racing seriously. But in 2019, I won my very first MTB race in India. It was then I decided to pursue it as a career, and I started training seriously. Soon after I had the chance to compete in the South Asian Games, but unfortunately, just a month before the race, I had an accident while training and broke my left wrist and suffered a knee injury as well. I still raced in the Games and won a silver medal.

When did you realise that you could make a living from the sport and when did you decide to take steps to make it happen?

2017 was the life-changing year for me. I left my job working in a school at the end of 2016 to look for work in the outdoor adventure sector. I took my trekking guide licence in the beginning of 2017. Later when the documentary on me was made, I was really inspired to push myself further in the sport. I was offered a job at Himalayan Single Track, a mountain bike tour company and bike shop in Thamel, when I didn't know much about the sport and the potential for a career in it. I learned so much from them, took the Level-2 British certification MBLA (Mountain Bike Leadership Award), did a few trips as a support guide, and the following year I was ready to roll as a fully qualified guide myself.

It is well known that in Nepal it is not as socially acceptable for young women to participate in sports as it is in western countries. What did your family think of your decision to pursue a career in mountain biking at that time?

It's definitely true that it's tough for women from Nepal to try making a career in sports, especially outdoor adventure sports. When I started mountain biking my family were not so concerned as I was still working as a teacher. Riding was just my weekend hobby. But they were quite shocked when I left my teaching job. They were concerned I'd given up a steady career and was then out riding all the time. They were mostly concerned about me finding a husband, as Brahmin women are normally married with a good husband in their twenties, but I wasn't ready for a husband and marriage (although I nearly got married when I was just 17, but thankfully the marriage was cancelled.) I was busy making my career. And I still am today! At family functions my family always ask when I am going to get married, it's a cultural and societal thing, but I won't be rushed until I meet the right person and will continue to compete and develop my career in mountain biking.

What do they think of your achievements in the sport now?

My parents and family are very happy with my achievements now. They see I've been improving, winning and travelling a lot, which none of them have done before. I feel proud of myself for proving them wrong, in a positive way. They openly support me now in whatever I'm doing, but my riding makes my mother worry a lot as I'm always in action in the mountains; and being a mother, she's always worried I might get hurt, which is a legitimate concern.

Has the recent rise in female participation and success in mountain biking made it more socially acceptable for girls to ride mountain bikes in Nepal today?

I would say so, yes. I can see mothers of our friends openly praising their daughter's achievements in the sport and sharing this news with their friends as well. But I also feel there's still some insecurity among the parents regarding women's safety, whether it's when they're riding alone or out on the trails. But definitely, it has become a lot more acceptable for women to ride bikes today.

What is the best thing about being a mountain bike guide?

You get to meet so many people from different backgrounds with different spirits and mentalities, and when you combine them all together, it can create unique moments of special bonding. It feels quite special when you're guiding people from around the world and you're in charge of their experience and helping them to fulfil their dream.

List your favourite three regions to ride in Nepal and why.

I would go with Upper Mustang, Annapurna region and Kathmandu.

Upper Mustang holds beauty and landscapes that are incomparable. It's hard to ride there as you'll be scaling many passes in one day; but the views, people and the riding take all of the pain away and soothes you with the surreal landscapes. Annapurna Region has always been a favourite region to ride since the first time I went there. There are many different landscapes, with the serious challenge of the Thorong La Pass (5416m), which gives such joy when you reach the top with your mountain bike. Kathmandu, the word itself is an emotion. I grew up there, learnt to ride there, and rode trails for the first time there. No matter how crowded and polluted it gets, it still holds a magic that no other region can replace. The whole riding community loves Kathmandu because the trails are easily accessible, there's never a dull moment riding around the

city, whether from the traffic, life on the streets or heritage sites and monuments.

Are there any Nepali regions you wish to ride, but have yet to explore on your bike?

I don't think I've travelled that much into my country yet. I've so many places I wish to ride one day. Among them, the Great Himalayan Trail (GHT) is the one I badly want to explore. And the far west region is also one of the regions I wish to discover in the near future.

You are going on a long ride into a remote region. What are the three most essential items you take with you in your backpack?

Essentials would be: warm clothes if it's cold, first-aid kit and medicines, as there's no good access to health care in remote areas, and definitely spare parts / maintenance kit for bikes.

Are the Nepali hills a safe place for women to ride?

A big YES! As a woman I find it super safe to ride around alone. Most of the people in Nepal are very friendly and are always there to help in any way they can. We Nepalese consider guests as a form of god, and it would be a sin if we disgrace our god.

If someone has a fear of getting lost in the Himalayas, it is a legitimate fear (that's why guides are always recommended), but if local people see foreigners are lost, they'll always help them. I've always found Nepal's remote hills safer than the cities. There should be no fear of getting robbed out in the Nepali Himalayas. Local people have the utmost respect for women, especially those who are foreign tourists, exploring their local areas. Locals get excited and welcome visitors and love to share and to listen to their stories.

Also, it's worth noting that the offline maps work perfectly fine in Nepal.

If you weren't a mountain bike guide, what would you most likely be doing?

I'd probably still be a teacher in a school. I still get offers to go back!

Why should people come and mountain bike in Nepal?

Nepal is a hidden paradise for mountain bikers. From busy cities to quiet and serene mountains, Nepal has everything to offer. Nepal isn't just Mount Everest – it has flat land, the Mid Hills and the high Himalayas. It is a place where you can have jaw-dropping views of 8000m+ mountains while riding your bike and feel the Himalayan vibes. People are happy and helpful, and the food is fresh and delicious. Plus, you get to ride with me and others from our fab and groovy Nepalese mountain bike crew. Come and ride with us!

Nishma Shrestha Girls Can Ride as Hard as Boys

Photo by N. Shrestha.

Nishma Shrestha is regarded as one of the most fearless female enduro riders in Nepal. Having grown up in a male dominated sport characterised by strong and courageous technical descent riding, Nishma has developed into a highly skilled enduro rider. Along with many domestic trophies and accolades, Nishma's greatest achievement was winning the gold medal at the 2019 Asian Games. Since then, Nishma has qualified as a UCI certified mountain bike coach and has set up her own mountain bike coaching company – Skills and Thrills, which focuses on technical skills training for all levels.

Did you have a passion for cycling from an early age? If so, tell us how it all started.

I was very shy when I was a young girl. I didn't know how to interact with people. I was not very social and I used to get very shy when I was in front of a lot of people but it all changed when my uncle took me for a short ride near my home in the place named Mudkhu. I learned how to ride a bike like other normal children in the neighbourhood. I used to borrow other kid's bikes to learn how to ride. In Mudkhu I got to meet with some of the professional riders. That place was a hub for mountain bikers where they used to hang out and talk about stuff. They were very welcoming towards me. They made me feel very comfortable in that environment and that's where I started my mountain biking journey.

You are regarded as a fearless enduro rider. Where did you find the courage to attempt technical and dangerous descents – was it something instinctive? Or did it develop over time?

To be honest, I am not a fearless person. I had to overcome a lot of those fears of riding technical and dangerous descents. It took me years to be the rider that I am today. It was not at all instinctive. I am not a natural talent – it was something that I had to learn and practice. I used to crash a lot in the early days! I was scared of riding off-road, downhill etc. I started riding as a cross-country rider, but in 2015 I made some friends who were doing downhill. I went riding with them. They used to practise a lot, making things perfect, they encouraged me to try some of those downhill techniques. In 2016 there was a national championship and I decided to participate in the downhill event. From that moment on I was hooked.

When did you realise that you could make a living from the sport and when did you decide to take steps to make it happen?

It was the time when I just graduated from high school and was about to begin my bachelor's degree. I had a lot of time on my hands, and I was riding a lot, travelling to various destinations around Nepal, making new friends and learning more about mountain biking and the opportunities in the sport. That's when I realised I could make a living from it. I was very interested in tourism, and mountain biking was something that was growing rapidly in Nepal. From 2017, I started working as a mountain bike guide in the peak season and participated in races in the off-season.

It is well known that in Nepal it is not as socially acceptable for young women to participate in sports as it is in western countries. What did your family think of your decision to pursue a career in mountain biking at that time?

My dad and my uncle were already in this industry, so I didn't have a hard time convincing my parents about pursuing a career in mountain biking. I used to ride a lot with boys, so whenever my neighbours saw me, they used to complain to my mum, saying that her daughter is riding alone with a bunch of guys, and asking what was I going to achieve by riding a bicycle? But my Mum was supportive and defended me from those critics and now I live my dream – riding, travelling, coaching and also making a living. But I guess I am one of the lucky ones, as many girls find it hard at the start to get approval from their families to ride.

Photo by N. Shrestha.

Has the recent rise in female participation and success in mountain biking made it more socially acceptable for girls to ride mountain bikes in Nepal today?

Mountain biking has not really been socially acceptable for either girls or boys in Nepal because it's hard to earn a stable income. And being an expensive sport, it is hard to maintain yourself as an athlete or rider. Even though the number of female riders is increasing, I think it is only really socially acceptable as a recreational sport, not as a career choice, as it's still not viewed as a serious career choice.

What is the best part of running your coaching company Skills and Thrills?

The best part is being able to share the skills I have learned to other riders who want to improve their riding techniques and help them be better riders. It's great seeing them trying to learn new skills and improve their riding abilities and techniques.

What are the main challenges of being a professional mountain biker in Nepal?

I have been trying to maintain myself, but it's not easy, because everything related to cycling is expensive and mountain biking is considered one of the most expensive sports. There is also a lot of mental stress. I always have to show my strong/tough side. I am always in fear that if I show weakness I might not be able to sustain myself in the sport. I am constantly compared with other people and their ability. I get judged by society and questioned a lot. Why am I riding with a lot of boys? Am I making money from the sport? But I try to keep a level head and make positive decisions based on my experiences and not on what other people think.

Where do you consider the best region for enduro riding in Nepal?

Recently, I rode in Dolkha and Phaplu (lower Solukhumbu). This region has the potential to become one of the best enduro riding destinations in Nepal. It's not only about the trails being developed in these destinations, but also about the diversity of the culture, traditions and ways of living. It's truly a unique experience.

Are there any Nepali regions you wish to ride, but have yet to explore on your bike?

I would love to explore more of the Langtang and Manaslu regions with my bike, as they're some of the best destinations for trekking.

Are the Nepali hills a safe place for women to ride?

I feel the Nepali hills are a safe place for women to ride. I have seen females travelling solo to various destinations. I myself travelled solo in 2017 with my bike and I was amazed to find out that people were really supportive and welcoming everywhere I went.

Mangal Lama Breaking the Barriers of What is Possible

Photo by M. Lama.

Mangal Krishna Lama was raised on a small family farm in Kakani in the hills to the north of Kathmandu and spent his early life working between school to help support his family through some difficult years. After moving to Kathmandu, he found work in a bike shop and began mountain biking. After entering a race in Sikkim, India, a love affair with adventure and travel began. Mangal became one of Nepal's elite mountain bikers over subsequent years, competing internationally in Malaysia, China, Bangladesh, Bhutan and Singapore as well as winning accolades at home. Following his racing years, Mangal co-founded a mountain biking tour company, El Yak, which he still runs today after navigating some difficult years since the 2015 earthquake and the Covid-19 pandemic.

It was during the pandemic that Mangal dreamed up the idea for the ultimate adventure challenge – to mountain bike across the mythical Great Himalayan Trail (GHT), a 1,700Km high altitude traverse of the Nepali Himalayas from Kanchenjunga in the east to Hilsa in the west, a feat that had never been attempted on a mountain bike, and widely considered impossible. In 2022, Mangal achieved his dream and rode the GHT high route solo, completing it in just 88 days.

How did you end up in Kathmandu, coming from a small family in rural Nepal?

I worked a lot at home on the farm with my father as a child, which was hard to balance with schoolwork. When I was 15, I failed my exams and I really panicked. I was afraid how my parents would react, so I ran away to Kathmandu and made my way.

How did you survive in Kathmandu being so young and naive to city life?

I knew how to work, so I was not afraid of that. I found a job as a builder's labourer and then a taxi driver, but they were not jobs that made me happy. I offered my services to a bike shop as a volunteer, and they took me on. It was there I learned bike mechanics and how to speak English with the foreign clients. Eventually they gave me a job.

When did you get your first bike?

I don't remember the year, but it was while I was working at the bike shop. I saved some money and got a loan from some family members. I really wanted to go and do a race in Sikkim. That was my goal.

You had some tough years with the 2015 earthquake and Covid. Did you ever consider giving up your dream to work elsewhere or return home to the family farm?

Yes, I did. After the earthquake I couldn't get work for two years. It was a nightmare. I considered quitting mountain biking to go and get a job in the Middle East, like so many Nepali men do. I also considered going home to the countryside, but there were no prospects there and my child was in school in Kathmandu, having a good education. So I decided to stick

at it, to stay in Kathmandu and keep riding, as I had dedicated most of my working life to mountain biking and the industry. I had come a long way, from nothing. It was one of the best decisions I ever made. I borrowed a small amount of money which helped my family get through this difficult time.

You are the first mountain biker to ride the GHT. What kept you going mentally during this phenomenal challenge?

Yes, I'm the first rider to complete that GHT high route. Some people have tried but didn't succeed, they quit in the middle of the trip. I was having a very hard time in Kathmandu at this time, and I wondered if I was the only person having a bad time. I wanted to see how people were coping up in the mountains. And when I heard about the GHT for the first time I wanted to know more about it. When I did some research I realised it was the challenge for me. I also wanted to give something back to the community, which I'm still working on at the moment.

You've ridden the length of the country' mountains. Which region do you have the fondest memories of?

Yes, I have ridden the length of the GHT, and the fondest memory of the trip was when

I arrived at the top of the Sherpani Col – a once-in-a-lifetime view, completely surrounded by mountains. It took my breath away. The Dolpo area is also staggeringly beautiful.

Are there any Nepali regions you wish to ride, but have yet to explore on your bike?

Yes, mostly the western part of the Nepali Himalayas. We still have a lot of things to discover there, including many spiritual places.

You are going on a long ride into a remote region. What are the three most essential items you take with you in your backpack?

Warm enough clothes (on the GHT I was carrying a very lightweight sleeping bag and a down jacket that didn't really help me when I was at 5000m. I couldn't sleep at night I was so cold). Also a GPS live tracking system so that others can see where you are, plus a satellite phone if you are really remote. Along with that some food, stuff to light a fire and a tent.

Some people are apprehensive to come to Nepal because of the high altitude riding, remote and hard to get to locations and the treacherous roads. What, from your experience, would you say to alleviate these concerns?

Is Nepal a safe place to ride?

If you are coming to ride in Nepal you should be trained physically, mentally and technically. Do your research. And before you plan to go to any specific remote areas, you should talk to someone who's travelled there recently, to get up to date information. If you plan well, Nepal is a very safe place to ride.

Photo by M. Lama.

Interviews

Interviews with international riders
who have contributed to raising the
profile of mountain biking in Nepal
to a global audience in recent years.

Phil Evans

Photo by P. Evans.

Phil Evans is an English mountain biker and adventurer and the founder of the world's highest mountain bike race, Nepal's Yak Attack. Phil has been visiting and working in Nepal for many years and has been one of the strongest advocates and supporters of Nepali riders breaking out into the international arena. Through his work with Yak Attack, Phil has played a key role in putting Nepal on the map as a global mountain biking destination for international riders.

What first brought you to Nepal?

I was in New Zealand and about halfway through an 18-month trip around Oceania when I stumbled across a talk on trekking in Nepal. I was really intrigued and 6 months later, after travelling through SE Asia, I jumped on a plane in Bangkok, Kathmandu bound. From the moment I stepped out of the taxi in Durbar Square, I just knew that I'd made the right decision!

How did the idea for the Yak Attack first come about?

During my second visit to Nepal, I happened upon an article on the Everest Marathon and was really drawn to the challenge. It took around 12 years to get around to entering the race, by which time I had been bitten by the mountain biking bug. Seeing the setup and logistics for the marathon got me thinking that Nepal would lend itself really well to a mountain biking stage race, and when I asked around it became apparent nothing like that existed. On returning to the UK, I contacted a handful of mountain biking companies in Nepal, found one that was interested in my idea and the rest is history.

Is it easy to do business in Nepal? Any tips?

I think we have been very fortunate over our 16 years of operating in Nepal. Apparently, not many small international companies last that

Photo by Corinne Evans.

challenging but the temperatures and altitude are not as extreme as the high mountains so you can have longer days in the saddle.

But for its mystique, wide open spaces and breath-taking scenery, Upper Mustang has to be top of my list. It's a place like no other I have visited, so far removed from the western world and even from the rest of Nepal. The riding is tough as you're above 3000m for the entire time and the terrain is dry and dusty but there's just something about this 'Forbidden Kingdom' that keeps calling me back.

How is Nepalese hospitality in rural and remote areas? Can foreigners expect a warm welcome?

Undoubtedly, Nepal has to be the friendliest place I have ever visited and I've been to a few! Most Nepalese outside of the cities live hand to mouth but they always welcome foreigners with open arms and will feed you and find you somewhere to sleep if you were ever in need. Most rural folk will only speak Nepali but the language barrier is not a problem when sharing time with people who are so full of joy and happiness. Payment would never be demanded but, of course, for somebody with such meagre means it would be greatly appreciated and only the

long. It's a cliché, but it really is a case of who you know in Nepal. We have been lucky to forge strong ties with many from the mountain biking community who have gone above and beyond to help us in times of need. To succeed in Nepal, you have to have a relaxed 'it'll be OK in the end' attitude because if you want to try to have total control over everything that is going on, you'll end up insane!

Which region of Nepal is your favourite to ride?

I really like the rural aspect of riding in the Himalayan foothills between Kathmandu and Pokhara, it's a side of Nepal not too many tourists experience. The terrain is incredibly most hardened and tight-fisted traveller wouldn't offer some form of recompense for food and lodging even in the most basic of settings.

Are there any regions of Nepal you have yet to discover on your bike, but would like to?

Due to being hands-on with Yak Attack every year, the majority of my riding in Nepal has been in the Annapurna region. I'd really like to head to far east Nepal and spend a couple of months exploring the trails around Hile, Ilaam and Tapeljung.

Has mountain biking in Nepal developed much since you first arrived? What key developments, if any, have you noticed?

Mountain biking has developed massively from when we first started Yak Attack in 2007. Then, there were only two or threeMTB shops with very basic supplies and only 5 – 10 serious riders. Now nearly every district of Kathmandu has its own bike shop with supplies to rival any western shop, with even quality e-bikes being available to buy or rent.

Participation in the sport has also increased 10-fold: with riders now competing in every category, XC, DH and enduro. Over the last two to three years, interest from female mountain bikers has also been growing. This is an area we have been working hard to improve and it's been heart-warming to see numbers grow from only 1 or 2 competitive females for many years to double figures in 2023.

Some people are apprehensive to come to Nepal because of the high-altitude riding, remote and hard to get to locations and the treacherous roads. What, from your experience, would you say to alleviate these concerns?

It's natural to be apprehensive when travelling to new places, especially one as exotic sounding as Nepal! Sometimes, you have to throw caution to the wind to experience real adventure and in Nepal you will find adventure around every corner.

If altitude is a worry, there's loads of lower level riding to do. Kathmandu to Pokhara barely exceeds 1000m in altitude but will leave you with memories lasting a lifetime.

The hardest places to get too are often the most rewarding. Allow plenty of time, take a local guide and embrace the whole journey as an adventure. If the road gets too treacherous for your liking (and many do), walk it, it'll soon get better, and if it doesn't, turn around, and walk back down it!

Nepal is the perfect place not to have too much of a plan, go with the flow and I guarantee you'll have the time of your life.

Sonya Looney

Photo by Kevin Trowbridge.

Sonya Looney is an American mountain biker from Albuquerque, New Mexico. Sonya has competed in ultra-endurance, stage racing, 24-hour, and 100-mile mountain bike races in a decade-long professional career. She has won world and national championships as well as some of the world's most gruelling mountain bike stage races, including Nepal's Yak Attack, Colorado's Breck Epic, The Brazil Ride, the Trans Andes and Colombia's La Leyenda. Today, Sonya is a health and performance coach, a motivational speaker and a mother. She also hosts her popular podcast The Sonya Looney Show. With two Yak Attack titles under her belt, Sonya knows well the remote terrain of Nepal and has been a strong advocate in encouraging international female riders to come to Nepal to break out of their comfort zones to try new challenges. Sonya's slogan speaks for itself: 'Be brave. Do epic shit.'

What first brought you to Nepal? How did the reality of being there for the first time compare to your preconceptions of the country?

I first came to Nepal for the Yak Attack Stage Race. Nepal was a perspective shift! The chaos was somehow manageable and made sense, the country has rich spiritual energy and the people were all very nice.

How do the Himalayas differ from other mountain ranges you've ridden across the world?

They are very dramatic, with a spiritual energy that is hard to describe.

Do you have a favourite memory or moment you can recall from your time riding in Nepal?

I enjoyed spending time in Manang. We took a day of rest and got to experience some time with locals and a slower pace to our adventure. Taking a mindful walk to soak everything in was meaningful.

How is Nepalese hospitality in rural and remote areas? Can foreigners expect a warm welcome?

People are excited to share their culture with you and may even invite you in for tea! Westerners can be distrusting of strangers, but you'd be missing out if you weren't open to rural hospitality!

From your experiences, do you feel rural Nepal is a safe place for female riders?

Yes! Both times I did the Yak Attack, I spent most of the race riding by myself. I never felt nervous or that I was unsafe.

What are the most essential items to take on a long ride into a remote region?

Gore-Tex jacket, bike tools and a water filter.

On your next trip to Nepal, which regions would you like to visit on your bike?

Upper Mustang!

Some people are apprehensive to come to Nepal because of the high-altitude riding, remote and hard to get to locations and the treacherous roads. What, from your experience, would you say to alleviate these concerns?

People are generally helpful. If you spend a few days to acclimate and gradually increase your elevation, it's easier to adapt. It's always uncomfortable to travel to a new place, but being curious and flexible will ensure you have maximum fun!

Cory Wallace

Photo by C. Wallace.

Canadian Cory Wallace grew up in the Canadian Rocky Mountain town of Jasper, Alberta, and currently races mountain bikes and gravel bikes around the World for the Kona Bicycle Co. Cory is a four-time World Solo 24hr Champion, multiple Canadian national marathon champion, owns the current FKT (Fastest Known Time) up Mt Kilimanjaro and around Nepal's Annapurna Circuit. He has competed in and won some of the most gruelling MTB races across the planet, including Nepal's Yak Attack, Bhutan's Tour of the Dragon, the Mongolian Bike Challenge, Australia's Wombat 100 and the Trans-Rockies. Despite these accolades, Cory is known as a low-key intrepid adventurer, and is a frequent visitor to Nepal.

What first brought you to Nepal? How did the reality of being there for the first time compare to your pre-conceptions of the country?

My first trip to Nepal was in March 2014 for the Yak Attack. The reality of being there for the first time was beyond my wildest dreams. The first time I saw a glimpse of the Himalayas it stopped my wheels in their tracks. This was during Stage 1 of the Yak Attack as we climbed out of the Kathmandu Valley. Currently in 3rd at that point of the race, I was soon passed by another rider as I was too busy taking pictures!

How do the Himalayas differ from other mountain ranges you've ridden across the world?

The size of them is unbelievable. Growing up in the Canadian Rockies, I thought we had big mountains, but the prominence of the Himalayas is basically double. The life in the mountains is something else which you don't find in many other mountain ranges around the world. The Nepalese have settled in the most hard to reach places and have built roads and trails all over the mountains, enabling easy access.

You have circumnavigated Nepal's mythical Annapurna Circuit four times in under 24hrs (a feat which normally takes the fittest riders multiple days). What drives you to achieve such extraordinary times?

Challenging myself keeps the spirits alive and well. The first attempt was just to try to finish under 24 hours, partly as a personal challenge, but also to show others what is possible. Since then, I've tried to lower my times each year, as it helps motivate me to consistently improve my practice and look at different ways to improve performance at high altitudes.

From all of your times riding in Nepal, do you have one memory that is the most vivid?

The first trip through the Annapurna Circuit was amazing. I remember being in the village of Chame at 2,700 metres, looking straight up at peaks on the Annapurna Massif hovering around 7,000 metres! Reaching Manang the next day and witnessing 8,000-metre snow-capped mountains out the front window was totally insane! Every time I head into the big Himalayas I'm blown away at the ruggedness and beauty of these giants.

List your favourite three regions to ride in Nepal and why.

Solukhumbu: Having spent four months of the Pandemic here, I was able to explore the area extensively. With trails, monasteries and quality tea houses all over the region it is a cyclist's paradise. Also being at the entrance to the Khumbu (Mount Everest) region gives it great access to a number of special areas.

Mustang: The riding around this dry area of Nepal is shockingly good, with trails hidden all over the mountain sides. Being in a touristy area with an airport, tons of teahouses and road access also means it is one of the few areas in Nepal with great infrastructure to have proper training camps. The mountains in this region are exceptionally stunning, and as a bonus it is also the gateway to the hidden kingdom of the Upper Mustang.

Kathmandu: The riding around Kathmandu is endless. It offers more options than almost any other big city in the world. Surrounding the city in a full 360 degrees are roads, trails, jungles, little villages, and some big hills to explore. Having spent three months of the pandemic here training while the roads were closed to traffic really made me realise just how much this city has to offer. The challenges are the pollution levels and traffic.

This makes it necessary to pick appropriate times and places to ride around the city depending on the season and current pollution/traffic levels. Once you get to know how to avoid the heavy traffic and find the quick ways out of the city, it turns into quite a rider friendly area.

Are there any Nepali regions you wish to ride but have yet to explore on your bike?

The mid hills region of Nepal is full of quiet roads, warm temperatures, and endless side valleys to explore. I would love to ride my gravel bike across this region to explore it more. Most people just think of the Himalayas when it comes to Nepal, but that is really only half of the country!

The far west looks untouched and ripe for exploration on a bike. The far east I have hiked around, the amount of roads and possibilities in this region are limitless.

Then you have areas like the Dolpa, Rara lake, and Terai. It's shocking how many options there are. These areas will become easier to explore once there is a bit more tourist infrastructure.

You are going on a long ride into a remote region. What are the three most essential items you take with you in your backpack?

1. Bike repair kit with tools to fix a flat tire and other common bike problems;

2. A cell phone with both sim cards (NTC and NCELL) and a battery pack to keep them charged between teahouses with power.

3. Food supplements such as whey protein, greens and some vitamins such as C, Bs and iron.

How is Nepalese hospitality in rural and remote areas? Can foreigners expect a warm welcome?

Nepalese hospitality in the rural and remote areas is as welcoming as any place I have ever experienced in the world. The locals truly seem to treat tourists as gods and are always there to ensure they can make your journey more pleasant in whatever way they can.

Some people are apprehensive to come to Nepal because of the high-altitude riding, remote and hard to get to locations and the treacherous roads. What, from your experience, would you say to alleviate these concerns? Is Nepal a safe place to ride?

To me Nepal is one of the safer places I have ridden a bike due to the access to teahouses and shops all over the place. In Canada when you go for a far-off ride, it's just you and Nature. You need to bring

everything to survive. In Nepal it is easy to pack light and find food and shelter every night along with multiple places to reload on food and water throughout the day. The majority of Nepalese riding is actually well below any real altitude (3000M). The treacherous roads are perfect for bikes as it's easy to pick lines between the rocks and other obstacles. It also slows down vehicles to a crawling speed, so you are usually passing them, not the other way around. Texting/distracted driving is a real problem in first world countries with good roads, but in Nepal it's virtually impossible, as the drivers have to remain focused at all times just to stay on the roads. I've had many more close calls riding in North America with vehicles buzzing by at 100km per hour than in Nepal.

Cory's three top tips for surviving on a bike in Nepal:

1. Have a good way of navigating with offline maps on your phone and the names of a few key places you're headed towards so the locals can point you in the right direction at the multitude of intersections.

2. Proper nutrition. Carbs are easy to find, but packing along some electrolytes, proper ride food and protein can help keep the energy levels optimal for the relentless hills you will cross.

3. Wear a helmet and stay aware of your surroundings, as there is never a dull moment out there!

Acknowledgements

Himalayan-sized thanks to... our guide, Om Adhikari, for his research and reconnaissance for both sections of The Road and for leading us safely across the entire country in great spirits. Many great moments shared.

To our support drivers, Binod on Section 1 and Sonam on Section 2 for their professional work and cool characters. To Manish Maharjan and Ananta Poudel for their epic photography, warm company, and great stories from their homeland.

To professional mountain bikers Christoph Sauser and Cory Wallace for their support, and for test-piloting The Road and giving the route some wonderful exposure.

To Ajay Pandit Chhetri, Usha Khanal and Chhimi Gurung for their help in piecing together the History of Mountain Biking in Nepal.

To the Graffeg Publishing team, particularly Joana Rodrigues, for putting together the pages of this book together so eloquently.

Special thanks to Mark Murphy, cartographer, for plotting and recording the entire route of The Road and for being a good friend and the best riding companion anyone could wish for.

Special thanks also to Jenny Caunt for writing the sections on the Peoples of Nepal, Ethics and Fitting In, Nepal's Seasons and Language, and for her belief in the project from the outset, her friendship and stellar organisation and route planning of the trip.

This book is dedicated to the memory of my parents: my Dad, Nigel, who taught me how to work; and my Mum, Shirley, who taught me how to dream.

Photo by Himalayan Single Track

The Road team (left to right):
Christoph Sauser, Jenny Caunt,
Cory Wallace, Richard Williams,
Om Adhikari, Mark Murphy.

Richard Williams
Author

Richard grew up on a farm in Pembrokeshire, Wales, and spent a number of years through the 1990s working in kitchens in Australia and teaching English around Asia. After a degree and master's degree in Development Studies from Exeter University and the LSE respectively, Richard worked as a technical writer at the Global Fund to Fight HIV/Aids, TB & Malaria in Geneva and later at the United Nations.

Some years later, Richard moved into the food business, creating Switzerland's Holy Cow! Gourmet Burger Company. More recently, Richard has enjoyed creative writing and has had three novels published by Graffeg, the most recent as part of the Books Council of Wales' Quick Reads series in 2023.

After a terrifying bus journey on the Leh to Manali Highway in 2000, Richard swore never to travel that way again, and invested in a mountain bike for all future mountain adventures. Since then, he has toured the mountains of Nepal and the Indian Himalayas a number of times and has participated in several stage races around the world, including Nepal's Yak Attack, Colombia's

La Leyenda del Dorado and the Swiss Epic.

After the 2015 earthquake in Nepal, Richard set up a foundation, Driftwood Association, focused on supporting rebuilding projects in remote Nepali schools, which he continues to run today. It was during these school visits on his bike that Richard discovered the beauty of the Mid Hills and developed the idea for The Road. All book royalties will go towards ongoing Driftwood projects. Find out more: @r_williams_books.

Jenny Caunt
Contributing Writer

Born in the UK, Jenny moved with her family to Australia when she was four and grew up riding bikes and horses in the Victorian countryside. After school, she chose to pursue a career as an architectural draftsperson. Towards the end of her studies, Jenny volunteered in a Red Cross soup kitchen and discovered her hidden passion and talent for cooking. Henceforth, she was drawn into making a career change to a chef. After 11 years in the industry, winning the Apprentice of the Year Award four times and working in some of Melbourne's top restaurants, she took off on a solo four-year journey to explore Asia and landed up in and fell in love with Nepal. Her discovery of Asian culture and the simple way of life made it hard to return to the grind of being a chef in Melbourne.

After meeting some local cyclists on a solo bike ride around Kathmandu Valley, Jenny developed a passion for the sport and then went into partnership with Santosh Rai to open Himalayan Single Track, a mountain bike tour company which has always put an emphasis on giving back to the locals and helping grow the mountain bike industry in Nepal. It is now one of the leading companies in Nepal for mountain bike tourism.

Still an excellent cook, as well as an art lover, outdoor traveller and cyclist, Jenny loves the culture of Nepal's backcountry and has had a long interest in the Mid Hills and opening up this region as a year-round tourist destination to a broader market of cyclist, rather than just focusing on the higher regions and their limitations.

During her 15 years in Nepal, Jenny has been involved in numerous races, rider training/coaching programmes and athlete development and facilitated the construction of Nepal's first and second asphalt pump tracks, built by Velosolutions/Pump For Peace.

Manish Maharjan
Photographer

Manish is an intrepid filmmaker and photographer from Kathmandu. After receiving a degree in Development Studies from National College, Kathmandu, Manish decided to follow his passion for bringing fresh perspectives to media platforms and went full time into camera work and

filmmaking. His earlier work focused on national TV shows that highlighted the struggle and rights of marginalised communities in Nepal, such as the Dalits and other ethnic minorities. Following this, Manish's work took him into the mountains, documenting the Prince of Bahrain's conquest of Everest with 16 of his royal guards.

Following this, in 2023 Manish took on a more ambitious project – documenting an attempt to conquer the world's 14 highest peaks over 8,000m by Norwegian mountaineer Kristin Harila and Tenzin Sherpa, a professional Nepali guide.

Documenting a second 14 highest peaks challenge is also underway for Manish, this time with a young Nepali climber, Nima Sherpa, who is hoping to break the record for the youngest climber to scale all 14 summits.

Inbetween his intrepid work, Manish enjoys covering biking events with his friends from the Nepali mountain biking community and making low-budget independent films. One of his collaborative film projects (with Ananta), a seven-part documentary, won the Imagine Nepal filmmaking award in 2022. Manish has summited Mount Everest as well as Mount Manaslu.

Ananta Poudel
Photographer

Ananta is a photographer, writer and creative director from Kathmandu. He is a co-founder of Pasa Production, where he dedicates his time to shaping pieces of art and breathing life into fresh ideas. Ananta finds joy in the small moments that unfold during his adventures around his homeland and strives to capture those fleeting moments and craft stories around them.

Recent projects include photographing the Yak Attack – the world's highest mountain bike race, which circumnavigates the Annapurna Himalayas, crossing the infamous Thorong La pass (5416m), and documenting the challenging Manaslu & Mustang Trail Races.

Ananta was a scriptwriter for the award-winning seven-part documentary for Imagine Nepal in 2022, which documented the lives of the Karnali people of Nepal and how they exist within their dramatic environment.

Despite being born and raised in the city, Ananta feels most at home travelling through and documenting the wilderness areas of Nepal.

Mark Murphy
Cartographer

Mark was born in the UK and as a child lived in Libya, Cyprus, Wales, Ireland and various parts of England. As an adult, he has lived in Kenya and for the past 25 years in Switzerland, working in the fields of design, print and publishing in both the private and intergovernmental sectors.

Mark first bought a mountain bike when in his 40s, to aid his recovery from a football-related knee operation, but it was only 10 years later that he actually took the bike off road! He joined Richard on a trip to Nepal for four days of MTB riding, visiting a number of outreach programmes supported by Driftwood Association. He fell in love with every aspect of the country and has returned many times, getting to know the friendly Nepali MTB community.

Aged 60, Mark embarked on The Road – proof that this epic cross-Nepal adventure is accessible to a wide range of people who seek an incredibly rewarding journey.